ENDORSEMENTS

Incisive, motivating, and applicable—Damon Friedman draws upon his military capabilities and life experiences as he empowers visionary leaders with practical insight and expertise as they embark on a mission to change the world. Igniting Movements *is a must-read for people driven to make an impact.*

Coach Bobby Bowden

Florida State University
Two-time NCAA football champion

Damon's desire is not only to be a transformer, but an igniter, and to see others carry that torch as well. Hence the book in your hands, Igniting Movements. *In this work, Damon communicates how movements really catch fire. First, he explores how they have ignited in history, then he creates a reproducible model, and finally he applies those insights to present day reality. And this is not just theory. He demonstrates how it has worked and is working in his growing movement/organization SOF Missions. Built on the vast wealth of experience he has leading special ops and humanitarian missions,* Igniting Movements *is pulsing with passion through every page. Damon's heart is to see lives transformed for good—both leaders and those whom they serve. This is a must-read!*

Professor Ryan Bolger

Fuller Theological Seminary

In Igniting Movements, *Damon Friedman, has laid out a path for any leader who wants to make a change in the world for the good. He walks the reader through pragmatic steps in how to ignite a movement, from finding your purpose to developing your strategy. I recommend this book for any reader wanting to make a difference.*

Chad Hennings

Former A-10 pilot, US Air Force
Three-time Super Bowl champion, Dallas Cowboys

Deep passions and vision drive us to leave our mark on humanity, but few of us ever see that come to fruition. The shortfall is often our inability to "ignite movements," to rally others into a shared passion and common vision to change the world. Special Operations Combat Leader Damon Friedman shares with us principles of leadership, ideology, organization, and strategy to organize individuals' collective gifts and talents in order to accomplish the seemingly impossible. A must-read for everyone who desires to leave a lasting impact in the world.

Chad M. Robichaux

Force Reconnaissance US Marine
Pro MMA champion
Founder and president, Mighty Oaks Warrior Programs

IGNITING MOVEMENTS

IGNITING MOVEMENTS

HOW CRITICAL FACTORS AND SPECIAL OPS EMPOWER WORLD CHANGERS

DR. DAMON FRIEDMAN

LT COL, USAF SPECIAL OPERATIONS (RET)

Advantage.

Published by Advantage, Charleston, South Carolina.
Member of Advantage Media Group.

ADVANTAGE is a registered trademark, and the Advantage colophon is a trademark of Advantage Media Group, Inc.

Printed in the United States of America.

10 9 8 7 6 5 4 3 2 1

ISBN: 978-1-64225-185-2
LCCN: 2019941914

Cover design by Carly Blake.
Layout design by Wesley Strickland.

This publication is designed to provide accurate and authoritative information in regard to the subject matter covered. It is sold with the understanding that the publisher is not engaged in rendering legal, accounting, or other professional services. If legal advice or other expert assistance is required, the services of a competent professional person should be sought.

Advantage Media Group is proud to be a part of the Tree Neutral® program. Tree Neutral offsets the number of trees consumed in the production and printing of this book by taking proactive steps such as planting trees in direct proportion to the number of trees used to print books. To learn more about Tree Neutral, please visit www.treeneutral.com.

TreeNeutral

Advantage Media Group is a publisher of business, self-improvement, and professional development books and online learning. We help entrepreneurs, business leaders, and professionals share their Stories, Passion, and Knowledge to help others Learn & Grow. Do you have a manuscript or book idea that you would like us to consider for publishing? Please visit advantagefamily.com or call 1.866.775.1696.

DISCLAIMER

The information herein does not imply official endorsement by the United States Department of Defense or its components.

CONTENTS

PREFACE

In 2010, I returned home from the Korengal "Death" Valley. Seven days of heavy combat in one of the most dangerous places on earth changed my life. It was a tipping point. After ten years of service, multiple deployments, numerous conflicts and explosions, I was suffering from a traumatic brain injury and post-traumatic stress. I was in a dark place and on the verge of losing my marriage and career. As a juvenile delinquent from the mean streets of Los Angeles, I found a way to survive. Twenty years later serving in the military's elite special operations, I found myself fighting for my life once again. This time, against myself: I questioned the purpose of my existence. It was quite an internal war, but I found hope. It was a miracle. Next, it was time to help others.

In 2011, my wife and I established SOF Missions, a faith-based nonprofit organization serving people across America. After multiple deployments in Iraq and Afghanistan, I have experienced the darkest hours of combat, knowing firsthand the struggles of veterans returning home. This led our team to create and produce the award-winning film *Surrender Only to One*, a faith-based film following real-life stories of elite combat warriors. Creating awareness was not enough though. Therefore, we established The Resiliency Project, a holistic program dedicated to helping veterans battle visible and invisible scars of war. Our mission is to help our warriors find their purpose, embrace resiliency, and live a life of wellness. Since the inception of SOF Missions, we have established groups and worked in various capacities throughout thirty-four different states, serving an estimated ninety thousand people.

Our national efforts were recognized by the Department of Defense and I was selected as the 2018 Spirit of Hope Award winner, named for entertainer Bob Hope, which "epitomizes the values of Bob Hope: duty, honor, courage, loyalty, commitment, integrity, and selfless dedication." I am passionate about making an atomic impact in the world. It took countless years and plenty of fails in order to find my ultimate purpose. This book is a genuine effort to pass on what I've learned and to help others find their purpose and ignite a movement.

The model presented in *Igniting Movements* comes from my doctoral studies. I researched movement theories, and over a hundred of past and present movements. In my dissertation, I crafted a Movement Rubric that groups movement characteristics into four categories: Human Agent, Ideology, Organization, and Strategy. Through the lens of this rubric, I conducted document reviews on select historical and contemporary movements, as well as semi-structured interviews with leaders of successful organizations across the country. I also conducted a document review on military special operations, which helped articulate practices and standard operating procedures. The research illuminates common critical factors that exist in each movement.

To learn how these factors can be applied in today's nonprofit world, I compared them to the current practices within SOF

Missions. I developed change initiatives and implemented them within the organization. The results have been outstanding! Our initiatives created a spark that ignited a small movement.

This research offers like-minded people an opportunity to implement critical factors in their organization, so they too can ignite a movement. *Igniting Movements* is a manual for those that have answered their God given calling and want to implement pragmatic practices that have brought success to thousands of nonprofit organizations. The common critical factors are keys to success. Each pillar is necessary and the synergy within each must exist. Obviously, there are the intangibles or what many call the "X" factors that can't be explained. However, this book is a blueprint, and, if you're serious about succeeding, *Igniting Movements* is the first step to ignition!

CHAPTER 1

FINDING YOUR PURPOSE

For the author of a book on igniting humanitarian movements and the founder of a nonprofit to say that he is an accidental humanitarian is a strange admission. But in my case, that's the truth.

I didn't set out to be a humanitarian, and I didn't know that it would end up being my true purpose in life. I spent the majority of my professional life working as a specialized weapon for the US military. I rose through the ranks of the Marine Corps and then transferred into the Air Force, where I served in Special Operations. I moved through a variety of roles and positions that changed the trajectory of the war against terrorism. I had a lot of power and authority: tactically, operationally, and strategically. I had all sorts of jobs, but the one that changed the way I view life was that of a Joint Terminal Attack Controller, or JTAC, which meant that my primary job was to coordinate bomb drops. I controlled half-ton bombs, usually from the battlefield, often in close quarters, and dropped them on the enemy.

Blowing bad guys to smithereens had a serious impact on me. As a soldier, I was consumed with a lust for the fight. The fight was my life and the only thing that made sense. I lived to kill villains. This probably sounds crazy, but I wasn't driven by bloodlust. My driving motivation was a love of country and the protection of its values, particularly liberty and freedom from oppression. My country had given me so much, and I wanted to give back.

I came from a troubled, impoverished home. As a kid, I was a juvenile delinquent, running wild in the streets of Los Angeles. I was a menace, terrorizing my own neighborhood with a baseball bat at times, though on the inside I was just a weak, scared kid rebelling against my own little life. I loathed myself, my abusive father, the junky apartments we grew up in—really everything. I was a nerdy kid, painfully timid, and unsure of myself. When you hate everything about yourself, you tend to hate everything about everyone and everything else too.

It took a long time to crawl out of the hole of my own mind and find myself. The short of it is that my country gave me a scholarship, an education, community, a sense of purpose, and ultimately a second chance. I owe everything to God and country. I joined the military, in part, as a way to give back to America. I wanted to protect the values of freedom, liberty, and resilient hope that this country was founded upon.

So I became a Spartan for my country. And I was good at locating, closing, and destroying the enemy. Really good. I took to bullets and bombs, finding satisfaction in the fight and a profound catharsis in channeling my inner rage, which had previously led me down a path of self-destruction. My anger, once misspent on terrorizing the neighborhood bully with a baseball bat, was now channeled into taking out actual terrorists, bad guys, and oppressors of men. I was fighting, literally *fighting*, for a better world.

While I will always be proud of my military service, I slowly became more interested in other ways of serving. As long as evil and injustice still hide in the dark corners of the world, there will always be a need for bullets and bombs. Someone has to defend freedom and liberty in the face of terror and oppression. But after a decade in active service, I was beginning to question whether I was still one of those people. While operating in Iraq and Afghanistan, we would embed with the local communities, earning goodwill through service, shows of good faith, and direct aid. I was finding this work just as fulfilling, and necessary, as nabbing bad guys.

There are many forms of oppression in this world, and not all of them can be fought on the battlefield. I was becoming less interested in bullets and bombs and more interested in books, bowls, and community bonds. Bullets and bombs can save people under immediate threat—but then what? To be free from oppression, people need more than their oppressors to be driven out. They also need education. They need ample food and clean water. They need infrastructure, medicine, and basic provisions. You cannot deliver a message of hope and freedom to someone who is sick and starving. Basic needs have to be met first.

And so, in 2011, my wife and I cofounded SOF Missions, an organization that conducted humanitarian missions throughout the globe. (SOF stands for Shield of Faith.) Though I was still on active duty, and often deployed, I started to organize and lead humanitarian missions while on leave from the military. I assembled a small team with several military guys and a doctor who treated the wounds I received in Afghanistan. We were a great pair: he was a genius doctor; I was a Special Ops officer with a strong background in logistics.

Mission work in the field seemed like a way we could come together to do some good in the world.

We just needed our first mission, which came when another organization informed us about a serious epidemic of malnutrition and viral outbreak among the Quilombolas, an indigenous people in the Amazon rainforest. The Quilombolas needed medicine and better healthcare. This seemed like the perfect joint venture for a doctor and a military guy to embed with a foreign community, so we jumped at the chance to help. We gathered a small team of volunteers and headed to Brazil. Over the course of ten days, we joined host humanitarians who were embedded in the community and helped set up several medical clinics. We treated hundreds of sick people.

This mission, though small, proved that I had something more to offer. My military experience and training allowed me to help people in need. The mission gave me time to reflect upon just how good my life was. I was depressed, questioning whether I really wanted to live, but seeing people with so little struck by such hardship made me realize how fortunate I am to be from a country that enjoys such abundance. We all have troubles, and I had mine, but they paled in comparison to the difficulties faced by these people—whom I had the power to help.

And help we did. SOF Missions continued to do humanitarian mission trips, one international and two domestic missions per year, and also conducted small projects in local communities. I recruited other guys from the military to help. We delivered aid, medical care, and disaster relief. We built schools and orphanages. We have operated in Brazil, Haiti, Honduras, Guatemala, Nicaragua, Costa Rica, Peru, Philippines, and more. We have provided professional medical support and education to a remote clinic in the mountains of West Virginia. We worked with the homeless and special needs community in New York City. We provided disaster relief in Louisiana. We were always looking for new ways to help, though my military career limited the number of missions I could lead each year.

A NEW MISSION, A NEW PURPOSE

A major turning point for SOF Missions, and me as its leader, came during a humanitarian operation in Peru in 2014. We raised more than $42,000 to build several orphanages. We were going to distribute a month's supply of food to a thousand people, primarily orphans, and provide medical care to hundreds more. It was our biggest mission yet. We recruited twenty volunteers, two of whom were from Special Ops—Green Berets, Purple Heart recipients, heavily decorated warriors—and they came with me to set up a medical clinic in the Andes Mountains. At one point, while we were climbing up the mountain, I looked to my left and right and saw these two men working hard to help others. They looked fulfilled and happy. It struck me then that we were not only helping others, but also helping ourselves.

Both of these men faced the typical challenges that veterans face. One in particular really struggled. We first met when he called me up out of the blue. He was alone in a room with a pistol loaded with a single nine-millimeter round when he called. For years, he wrestled with PTSD, which was the primary reason why he departed the military. He was in his mid-twenties, homeless, and out of hope. He was almost ready to end it all, but a mutual friend gave him my phone number and urged him to call me.

I listened to his story. He told me how the people he shot and killed haunted his dreams and his waking life alike. He told me about friends he had seen shot dead or blown up in front of him. He himself had been blown up and shot. Buildings collapsed on him. He was in physical, mental, and spiritual pain. He was out of hope and ready to end it all.

This was a story I knew well, having lived it myself. Combat leaves scars, and not all of them are physical. Even when you don't come home wounded, or, worse, in a body bag, war changes you. By 2010, shortly before founding SOF Missions, I deployed to Iraq and Afghanistan multiple times. My most harrowing experience was when my unit came under siege while closing down a US base in the Korengal Valley, known as "The Valley of Death" among the American forces because so many of us lost our lives there. We were actually there to shut the base down, but the enemy started to emerge from the valley in wave after wave. For seventy-two hours straight, we were literally fighting for our lives.

I survived, but the ordeal changed me. I came back home not only wounded, but also confused and agitated. I was in pain—not just physical and emotional pain, but also spiritual pain. All my problems were catching up with me. I was dealing with—or, more accurately, trying *not* to deal with—the aftermath of war and suffering from symptoms of post-combat stress, as well as the lingering scars of growing up in poverty with an abusive father. I wasn't handling any of it well. My sleep was troubled. My anxiety and stress levels were through the roof and I experienced several flashbacks. On the verge of my own total self-destruction, I was sabotaging my personal life and my career. I was drinking heavily to numb the pain. I was fighting with my wife. I was jeopardizing my military career. The things that mattered most to me were slipping through my fingers.

Despite all of my accomplishments, I was very insecure. I rose up the ranks in the military, but I still had low self-esteem. I was tired of trying to prove myself. It wasn't making me happy and didn't seem worth it. Struggling in my career, my marriage, my day-to-day life, with symptoms of posttraumatic stress—*nothing* seemed worth it. There came a point when I started to question my will to keep on living.

But I did find healing. After returning from the Korengal Valley in Afghanistan, I saw a lot of medical specialists, including the doctor who would be the first to join me in SOF Missions. He helped me through that healing process, not just the physical healing, but the mental and spiritual healing as well. While reevaluating my life, I came to the realization that I was too self-focused. My whole life was shaped by a relentless need to prove myself. I was always focused on the next rank, the next medal, more recognition, more validation, more, more, more. But no achievement was ever enough. It was all for me, and none of it brought me lasting peace.

Inspired by how my doctor helped me, I started to wonder: what would my life look like if it were about helping other people rather than just myself?

I decided to turn my passion and drive outward and work for others for a change. In doing so, I found personal healing. Fast forward several years, and I had multiple humanitarian missions under my belt. I was no longer asking myself whether life was worth living. On the contrary, I was *thankful* to be alive. Helping others felt good and worthwhile, and I wanted to do it more. I also wanted to bring the message of hope, which saved me, to others. I wanted to empower people, help them heal, and spread that message of hope.

This was what was running through my head while I was on the phone with the veteran who called me out of the blue to say that he was going to kill himself. When he was done telling me about his problems, I told him I had been there too and that there was hope on the other side. I wanted him to know that healing was possible.

"Put the gun down," I said. "You can't shoot yourself; God put you here on this earth for a purpose."

We talked for a while, and he listened. He put the gun down. He decided not to shoot himself, at least not right then.

"All right," he said. "What do I do now?"

We met up and spent time together. We talked and worked through his problems. I invited him to join us on humanitarian missions, and he agreed, thus starting a journey of mental and spiritual healing. He started using his God-given skills to make the world a better place, finding a new life and a greater purpose in helping others.

Not a year later, we were trudging through the Andes together on our mission in Peru, and I just looked at him and saw how far he had come. From broken, homeless, and suicidal to a life of fulfillment and purpose. He was healing himself by helping others. This veteran called me with a gun in hand, telling me he wanted to end his life, and here he was, not a year later, doing good work and smiling the whole time. The transformation was miraculous.

A sudden epiphany donned on me there on the mountain: we, as warriors, were doing all of this service to help others in need—but who was there to help us? There are millions of struggling veterans. The Department of Veterans Affairs National Suicide Data Report of 2016 found that over twenty veterans commit suicide every day in this country. That's nearly a suicide every hour of every day, all year 'round. There aren't enough people and systems to help veterans, and they keep falling through the cracks. Right then it struck me: what if I—what if we—did the same thing for our own brothers in arms as we were doing for others? What if we worked to help one another? I wanted to do something. I wanted us to be able to help each other, and in so doing find a renewed sense of purpose and healing.

My true purpose became clearer to me that day. Not only did I know that I wanted to help veterans—in addition to the widows, orphans, and impoverished populations we were already working with at SOF Missions—but I also realized that my passion was empowering other people to find their purpose too. We all have a purpose in this world. Every time a veteran, or anyone else, commits suicide, the world loses not only a life, but also all of the good those people could have done if they pursued their purpose. Every death is a shame—but the real tragedy is the life not lived. When people get to fulfill their ultimate purpose in life, they not only enrich their own lives, they also enrich the community and, in turn, the world.

I am just one person, and I cannot help everyone, but by helping my own community of veterans and empowering them to find purpose, they can pay that forward and do better. As of the writing of this book, 2.7 million veterans have already been deployed to either Iraq or Afghanistan, often both, since 2001. Many of them are struggling with the aftermath of being at war. I wanted to know what it would look like if SOF Missions helped them all heal—physically, mentally, and spiritually. What would they be able to accomplish in the world?

I made it my mission to find out. Because helping veterans is my passion. Encouraging people to find their own passion and purpose, and actually executing on it, is my purpose. This is why SOF Missions has been shaped and built: to empower veterans to find their purpose and help others.

That is also why I am writing this book. I want to empower other people—not just veterans—to start their own organizations so that they can find, and realize, their purpose and calling. But before you can build an organization, start a movement, and change the world, you first have to decide what your mission is. That mission shouldn't be just anything. It should be your true calling. SOF Missions only really started to take off once I was following my true purpose.

FROM ORGANIZATION TO MOVEMENT

My epiphany on our trip to Peru in 2014 was a turning point for SOF Missions. Up until then, we focused on small humanitarian missions and local projects. When we started in 2011, SOF Missions was just a handful of people working on a single team. We grew slowly over the next few years. By 2014, when we went to Peru, we put together team of twenty volunteers—but it was still just a single team.

Once we switched our focus to helping veterans, and empowering them to help others, we began to grow. I am only one person. I can only undertake so many humanitarian missions per year. By having other veterans run their own SOF teams we could do far more. SOF Missions is now a decentralized network of teams all across the country. At the writing of this book, there are twenty-five SOF teams and counting, and SOF Missions has served some eighty thousand people globally.

These groups are run by veterans or those who support them, but that doesn't mean that they are working on veterans' issues. Each group has its own purpose and mission near and dear to the hearts of the people that organized the team. Each team is locally based, for the most part, and while many are working on veterans' issues, they focus on different causes and populations. Some teams work on helping veterans find housing, as there are forty thousand homeless veterans living on the street or camping in the woods on any given night. Other groups are dedicated to suicide prevention in veteran populations. One team works only with female veterans. Some are purely support groups and don't conduct missions or projects. Other teams aren't working on veterans' issues at all, but are simply working to strengthen their communities or helping other groups.

My own team still works in the field doing humanitarian missions. We still do construction projects, helping to build schools, orphanages, and infrastructure. We distribute food, especially to orphans and widows. We set up medical clinics. Those are my passions. Other teams are led by different people with different purposes. Our new structure empowers veterans to pursue their own passions. We have different passions because we have different backgrounds. I've always cared most about helping children, orphans, widows, and veterans. This is largely due to my background. I am a veteran. I was a child who went through a rough childhood and was raised by a single mother.

I care about other causes, of course, but they aren't my passion, which is why it's best for me to empower other people to pursue theirs. No one person can do everything. No one team can do everything. No single organization can do everything, for that matter. Everyone has something to offer, but that something is different. The structure of SOF Missions embraces our team leaders' and members' different skills and passions to do more good.

And that is why the new incarnation of SOF Missions is so powerful. We are a global network of teams, mostly run by veterans, pursuing a diverse range of projects and missions.

In his 2009 book, *Movements That Change the World*, Steve Addison fully and succinctly defines movements as:

> *...informal groupings of people and organizations pursuing a common cause. They are people with an agenda for change. Movements don't have members, but they do have participants. The goals of a movement can be furthered by organizations, but*

organizations are not the totality of a movement. A movement can have leading figures, but no one person or group controls a movement.

This is very distinct from an organization, which is merely a structured body of people with a particular purpose. The organization is *not* the movement. They are not interchangeable. The movement transcends the organization; no one leads a movement. These are critical distinctions.

In the case of SOF Missions, the national organization is not the movement. Damon Friedman is not the movement, nor are any of our staff. We are *in* the movement, but so is everyone who volunteers, helps, receives help, and goes on to help others. Our donors are part of the movement, as are our many advocates and champions. The movement is the collective engagement of everyone involved and affected. These people are impelled to act by the ideology set forward by the organization, and often guided by the organization's strategy, but the people themselves are the movement, not the organization. The movement can survive even if the organization disappears and another takes its place, allowing organizations that are successful at igniting a movement to leave a legacy and contribution that outlives them.

While an organization is not a movement, organizations can help drive and *ignite* a movement. Ignition is the goal of an organization trying to start a movement. Ignite means to set fire, but it also means to give life or energy to something. Ignition means to set in motion. That is what successful organizations do: they set the world on fire with an idea that resonates with people. Those people are the movement. The organization can set this in motion, but the movement either ignites or it does not. The organization can help light the torch, but it is up to the movement to carry the torch. The movement, and the leader for that matter, is just the tinder, not the fire.

In his book *The Tipping Point*, Malcolm Gladwell defines the tipping point of a social movement as "that magic moment when an idea, trend or social behavior crosses a threshold, tips, and spreads like wildfire . . . the moment of critical mass, the threshold, the boiling point." This is the moment of ignition, put eloquently into words. Gladwell likens the phenomenon to a virus that spreads through the community. Whether you prefer the imagery of a virus or a wildfire, the idea is the same: the spreading of an idea or ideology through social contagion. At this moment of ignition, when the spark catches fire, a movement is born, and while that movement is borne of an organization, the movement takes on a life of its own.

The point of this book is to help people ignite movements. Creating an organization is only part of that process. In later chapters, we will discuss how to create an organization, lead it and garner followers, develop and propagate a consistent ideology, and develop and execute a strategy that will allow you to achieve your mission. But all of this, including the organization itself, is in service of igniting a movement. The organization and the leader are always in service of the movement, not the other way around.

What has made SOF Missions so successful in the last few years is that the organization is structured in a way that fosters movement building. We encourage those we help to get involved by starting or joining a team. We are changing one life at a time through our initiatives, and many of those people go on to help others, creating a compounding effect that ripples out and through communities.

WHAT'S YOUR PURPOSE?

SOF Missions, at the national level, does not give orders or assign missions to the local SOF teams that make up the movement. Our mission is to empower veterans to find spiritual healing by pursuing a sense of purpose. We don't care what that purpose is as long as it conforms to the movement's goal of helping others and making the world a better place. My purpose is to help veterans find theirs. That's my goal. I want them to find and work toward their purpose, not mine.

I work with widows and orphans because those causes matter to me. Those are *my* passions. That's *my* purpose. The people who have started other SOF Missions teams have their own passions, and we encourage them to follow their own sense of purpose. We are proud to have them do so under the SOF banner. And when our veterans realize their purpose and find healing in working to make it a reality, we in turn realize ours. This book is an extension of that goal. I want to empower you to seek out your purpose. I want to help people launch organizations that can ignite movements. The goal is to make the world a better place.

Veterans, orphans, widows, those in abject poverty: these are causes that keep me up at night, along with a burning desire to empower others to help. That's just me though. You have to figure out what keeps *you* up at night. That's the only way you will be able to muster the drive and courage to stick with the cause when things get rough. Running an organization is hard. You will abandon the cause when things get tough if you don't truly believe in it. If you're going to dedicate your life to something, it has to be your true purpose.

I studied movement theory and mission work while pursuing my doctorate in Intercultural Studies from a prestigious institution in California. When I arrived on campus, my professor asked us to get out our focus papers (a one-page paper roughly describing what you wanted to study for your doctorate).

"I want to just ask this question right now," he said. "What keeps you up at night? If that's not the topic of your focus paper, I want you to crumple it up right now."

The class looked at each other, to see if anyone did so, and then back at the professor. We didn't know if he was serious.

"Go on," he said. "Crumple them up. If that's not what keeps you up at night, toss it in the garbage. This is going to be your academic contribution to the world. It needs to be your passion. If it's not, you're wasting your time. Don't waste the next four years of your life."

I clutched my paper close to my chest. Though only a single page, the paper represented a solid month of work. I wrote and rewrote that one page about a hundred times. When they accepted me into the program on the strength of my paper, I assumed that it was good. And it *was* good. But, reading it over again that night, I had to admit that the topic wasn't what kept me up at night. Reluctantly, I crumpled up the topic paper and sat down at my computer to start over. I typed up a whole new focus paper that night, a crude rough draft, though I was much happier with the new version when I finally went to bed in the early hours of the morning.

The next day, I handed the new draft to my advisor. "This is what keeps me up at night," I said.

"Good," he said, without even looking it over. "Whatever it is, that's what you're going to write about."

My new research topic, as you might guess from the subject of this book, was about how to ignite a movement. I wanted to study past movements to see what they shared in common. I wanted to know how movements were born. My passion was not embedding in the community, as important as that is to mission work. My passion was empowering people to pursue *their* passions. My passion was helping people change the world. I wanted to study movements and learn what caused them to ignite. I wanted SOF Missions to ignite a movement. I wanted to help other people ignite movements of their own. My research, along with this book, is the culmination of that passion. I wanted to create a handbook that would help other people pursue their own sense of purpose by founding organizations that can ignite movements. My ultimate goal was to create a sort of manual that would empower other people who wanted to change the world. *That* was my passion. That was my purpose, and that was what kept me up at night.

Dissertations are a huge undertaking, but they pale in comparison to founding a successful organization. Building an organization that can ignite a self-sustaining movement with the power to change the world for the better is a Herculean task. You won't make it, and neither will the organization, if your heart isn't in it 110 percent.

This isn't to discourage you from following your heart. On the contrary, I am saying the opposite—*go follow your heart.* That's the only way you're going to be an effective leader who can run an effective organization. I want you to succeed over the long haul. Which means you can't just do anything—you have to find your true purpose.

If you don't know what your purpose is, then perhaps you're not ready to start an organization of your own. That doesn't mean you won't ever be able to do so, you're just not ready yet. Go out and experience more of the world. Find your people and help them. Join organizations and movements that interest you. Get your hands dirty helping other people? It is only by helping that you will discover how you want to help. Get out there and help others, and you will find your purpose in due time. And, in the process, you will learn how to enact change. Thoughts and feelings don't change the world—actions do.

What specific cause you choose ultimately does not matter as long as it is a true passion. Successful movements tend to focus on a specific population and cause. "A mission set," as we called it in the military, involves a target population, a project, and/or a cause. The mission set can be, and often should be, narrowly defined. Your purpose will be to help whatever population of people you really care about by addressing a specific cause that matters to you. Do not be afraid to keep your mission narrow. If your passion is to help people in your neighborhood, go make your neighborhood a better place. If your cause is to build a better park or a community center, go out and make it happen.

Small causes are worthwhile—when you reach your objective, you can always take up another cause. You don't have to do everything yourself. The world needs all types. Just as no one person can do everything on his or her own, and no one team can accomplish everything, no one movement can address all people and all issues. SOF Missions has been about empowering veterans to find healing and change the world. Veterans have a lot to offer, but so does *everyone*. Every person has a unique set of skills, talents, and passions and purpose in life. While I have been focused on movement building in the veteran population, I also want to help empower anyone to build a successful movement.

To that end, I have written this book to help people start their own organization that can ignite a movement that changes the world. This book is not specific to veterans or any other single cause. Instead, we will be exploring successful movements across history. SOF Missions is only one example of an organization that is igniting a movement, and we are far from the pinnacle of a movement. We still have a lot of growth ahead of us. But we have succeeded as an organization. We have reached the point of ignition.

This book is about movement building. We will be looking at the common factors that are shared by many organizations researched during my dissertation, as supported by a historical analysis of movements across time. The goal of this work is to help you build and lead your own organization that might one day ignite a movement of its own.

But, first, you have to figure out what your purpose is. You have to recognize your superpower. You have to figure out what keeps you up at night. This is something I cannot do for you. You have to look deep into your heart, and deep into your spirit, and identify your cause or causes.

What I can tell you is this: hope is always about overcoming oppression. We all want to change the world in our own specific ways, but they boil down to the same things. And those things are, invariably, liberty and freedom from oppression.

Though oppression comes in many forms, we resist them all in the same ways. The ideology that drives me to fight for freedom and liberty in the US military is the same ideology that guides my humanitarian work. In both cases, I go out on missions to free people from oppression. In the military, I am fighting literal human oppressors who terrorize both people in the Western world as well as their own communities in Iraq and Afghanistan. We work with local communities to free them from an evil ideology that would oppress them and use their bodies for evil. We want to set them free. The people of Iraq and Afghanistan no more support ISIS or Al Qaeda today than they supported Saddam Hussein or the Taliban in the past. Of course, *some* people do—and those people are the oppressors we are fighting against to lessen human suffering and make the world a better place.

These are the same things that I want out of my humanitarian missions. The oppressor isn't always a man with a gun, a whip, or a shackle. Abject poverty is just as oppressive as any dictator. Hunger is an oppressor. Homelessness is oppressing. Disability can be oppressing. Natural disasters are oppressing.

And then there are also human oppressors whom you can fight without needing the full might of the US military at your back. Human traffickers are oppressors. So are thieves, corrupt politicians, gang members, bullies, and other people who would tread on the freedoms and liberties of others.

And then there is self-imposed oppression, which is much of what we fight at SOF Missions. Sometimes, we are our own worst oppressors. PTSD and other traumas are oppressing. Addiction and the kind of emotional suffering that leads to suicidal ideation are oppressors. So are bulimia and anorexia, anxiety, depression, and self-harm. We are good at coming up with ways to oppress ourselves.

Whatever your cause, get out there and work to end oppression. Help people find salvation and redemption. Make the dream of transformation a reality for people who need your help, whatever that looks like.

CHAPTER 2

ON PRAGMATISM: WHY HOPE, DRIVE, AND FAITH ARE NOT ENOUGH

Knowing your purpose can be a powerful and liberating feeling. I experienced a catharsis when I realized my higher calling and that my primary purpose was helping others. When I was in Peru and had my epiphany about empowering veterans to help each other, it was like a light flicked on in my head and a fire ignited in my heart. There is no high like knowing your ultimate purpose.

After that kind of realization, many people are ready to dive head first into their mission. You may want to start doing projects and missions right away. You may feel ready to go, powered by an unbounded hope, a burning sense of drive, and an unfailing sense of faith. This may feel very natural to people who inherently have a lot of initiative and a can-do attitude.

Trust me, I get it. I have dedicated my entire life to spreading a message of hope. My faith guides me above all else. And I have always been driven, whether it was to escape poverty, blazing the track in college, climbing the ranks in the military, or building SOF Missions to be a top-notch nonprofit organization working with veterans. My entire purpose in life is based around my faith in God. I understand both the power and the almost intoxicating effect of hope, drive, and faith.

Hope, faith, and drive are critical to any large endeavor, including founding and running an organization. I believe that hope is a prerequisite for even getting started. From a Christian perspective, hope is a desire for something we are certain to receive, an assurance concerning the future. At SOF Missions, we work hard to instill a sense of hope in veterans. Finding hope is an essential part of their spiritual healing. You cannot have a sense of purpose without hope. Without hope, people are lost and adrift. You need to hope in order to even *start* starting a movement.

Drive is the determination to put in time and effort. We are talking about a willingness to shed blood, sweat, and tears for the cause. Good leaders show grit and endurance in the face of adversity. This is essential for any leader. You will eventually encounter obstacles and setbacks, probably sooner than later. Success is not just about avoiding problems and complications—it requires you to work through problems as they arise. You need the internal energy to keep moving forward over the long haul, and drive is what keeps you going. Some people are born with drive, while others learn to cultivate a better work ethic and a can-do attitude.

Faith is what will see you through when things get hard. Even the most driven people sometimes lose hope. When you can't see the road in front of you, when it seems like there is no way out, when the odds are against you, hope can be in short supply. When I was fighting in the Korengal Valley in Afghanistan, controlling exploding munitions for seventy-two hours straight, I started to break down. This was the longest I had ever been awake. I was positioned at an operational post, identifying the enemy and relaying their coordinates, making sure it was safe to drop bombs in close proximity of our own troops. The slightest mistake could have meant killing someone on my team. The slightest delay or hesitation might have meant that the enemy would kill them instead. The pressure was constant and intense. My body and mind were failing me. By day three, I was hallucinating from sleep deprivation. I smack myself from passing out or seeing double.

I didn't know how long I could go on in that way. My hope started to falter, and so did my drive. Man only has so much endurance. It was my faith that I leaned on then. I reached out to God and prayed for him to see us through safely. A sense of serenity descended over me and I felt buoyed by a renewed vigor. I understand that not everyone believes in God and not everyone believes in miracles. But, from my perspective, the battle suddenly turned, and there was no explanation except divine intervention. My bomb drops went off with precision. My guys' bullets hit with hair-splitting accuracy. It was like the hand of God was guiding our rounds. The enemy soon retreated back down the valley.

My faith is what saw me through that ordeal, allowing me almost a superhuman strength at a time when I was so tired that I barely even felt human. You don't have to be religious to have faith. You just have to believe and trust in something *greater* than yourself. For me, that's God.

I would not be able to maintain hope, drive, and faith were it not for my unflinching belief in my mission. My sense of purpose is what keeps me going in hard times and the wellspring from which I derive my faith. This is why finding your purpose is so important. If you don't focus on the things that keep you up at night, you will lose hope, your faith will falter, and your drive will evaporate. You need hope, drive, and faith as the leader of an organization. All three are mission critical.

However, as important as they are, hope, drive, and faith are not enough. While you have to have hope that things can be better, the drive to go make them better, and the faith that your work will make a difference, these alone will not sustain an organization, much less ignite a full-fledged movement. You may feel ready to take on the world, even save the world, armed with just your own grit and determination, but this is a mistake. You're going to need more than hope, drive, and faith. You're going to have to slow down in the name of pragmatism.

THE POWER OF PRAGMATISM

If hope, drive, and faith were all you needed to ignite a movement, I would not be writing this book. There are a million books, many of them great, about hope, drive, and faith. But these are not enough to change the world. If they were all you needed to ignite a movement, many more nonprofit organizations would succeed. Exact failure rates are elusive, since small and young organizations are hard to count and don't always gain or even seek 501(c)(3) status before collapsing. The oft-quoted 90 percent figure, while perhaps true, isn't actually based in any studies, but the sad truth is that the vast majority of nonprofits fail, most early in their existence.

Organizations don't fail because their leaders didn't *want* to succeed. They often don't fail just because the leaders didn't try. Most often, they fail because the leaders didn't try the *right* things. People who want to start movements have a lot of passion and drive, which all too often means that they are short on patience and practicality. Too many people launch head first into a mission without knowing what they are doing. Passion, drive, and even a good idea for an underserved population or cause that people care about won't get you very far if you're not pragmatic.

Effective leaders should be pragmatic. Hope, drive, and faith are important. You need to have a message of hope, the drive to get things done, and the faith that you can make a difference. But you will need more than hope, drive, and faith—you also need a *plan*.

You need to understand what makes an organization work and how to operate one. Organizations are complex machines with lots of moving parts and people pulling the strings. It is up to you to lead those people, which requires actually knowing something about leadership. You need to know how to communicate your mission to the followers and donors who make up your movement. You need to know how to keep a group working together. Without internal unity, an organization will eventually fail, whether by spectacular collapse or slow attrition. Organizations, like businesses, have to be efficient and efficacious to survive. Otherwise, the organization will get bogged down and eventually fail. You can only run an organization inefficiently for so long before you fold or someone else comes along and does it better than you.

Struggling through your own incompetence and ignorance is needless and counterproductive. You will spend so much time, effort, and resources putting out fires that you won't be able to thrive or grow. This will not only impede the mission, but you will lose your hope and faith, and your drive will eventually dissolve. Followers will start to abandon the movement, and you can't just power through on your own forever. Having hope is easy, but *keeping* hope is hard when you don't have a solid plan for what you are going to do. Finding the drive to get started is easier than maintaining drive over the long haul. You won't be able to keep up the energy if you are struggling against your own organization's ill-conceived structure or incoherent strategy. The grind will eventually get to you. Ultimately, it is only a matter of time before you lose faith and abandon the mission altogether.

Failure from attrition is actually the *best*-case scenario for poorly structured organizations and ill-prepared leaders. More often, the whole endeavor implodes before it ever really begins. Working around a lot of passionate and ambitious people, I see this all of the time. People jump head first into a mission without laying the groundwork or doing their homework first.

In the early days of SOF Missions, we once teamed up with a person who wanted to do a humanitarian mission in a poor country in Central America. The mission had multiple parts. He wanted to provide food, medical aid, and other necessities to indigenous communities in the countryside. He also wanted to construct a community center. Though he hadn't done humanitarian work before, he was enthusiastic. I was teaming up with him to show him the ropes. Everyone has to start somewhere, so I agreed to help out with the first mission.

The mission was a catastrophe. He was even less prepared than I could have imagined. His heart was in the right place, and he truly believed in the mission, but he was not ready for the work. He wanted to help the local indigenous community, but he didn't know the first thing about the culture. No one in the community trusted him, it was hard time getting them to communicate their needs. We didn't even know what they needed from a community center, or if they even needed one at all, but we were trying to build one. I emphasize *trying* to build one because very little construction actually took place. This well-meaning do-gooder hadn't built anything in his life, nor had anyone else on the team. What's more, there wasn't enough money for the construction project. He didn't know how to raise financial donations or communicate the potential impact of the mission to interested donors, so we ran out of funds.

The whole project was doomed from the start. He hadn't prepared at all. Not only did he lack crucial knowledge and skills, he was completely unaware of his gaps. He hadn't even bothered to think about what he needed to know or do to prepare. So our team arrived as scheduled with supplies and tools in hand, but no actual plan. It never even occurred to him to learn about the indigenous culture. He didn't consult or team up with anyone in construction or engineering before trying to build a complex community structure. He didn't bring on others who could compensate for his gaps in knowledge because he wasn't aware of the gaps.

Don't be like that guy. His heart was in the right place, but he was simply not prepared. All of the heart—all of the hope, drive, and faith in the world—won't save your mission if you go in unprepared. Before dragging your whole family to a foreign country to "help" the community, you might want to study the culture first, whether that community is an indigenous society in the Amazon or the homeless veterans living on the streets of New York. This becomes more important the further you go from home. Don't fly into a foreign country without learning the culture, laws, and regulations. The more foreign the culture and location, the more preparation you need to do. Learn about the people. Learn the local laws, customs, and regulations. Learn the language! Not only will this help with practical operations, it will also help build goodwill. No one will take you seriously if you can barely say hello or goodbye in the local language. If you think you're going to be putting up buildings, you might want to learn something about construction beforehand or find an experienced contractor or engineer. If you want to fund a charitable cause, you need to learn about fundraising.

This is basic stuff, but sometimes passionate people get caught up in their own aspirations and tripped up by their haste. Temper your passions enough to slow down and act pragmatically. Passion is good, necessary even, but don't let it keep you from taking the time to plan.

You can't just show up somewhere and expect to start serving people without learning about what they need and how to render those services. Aspiring actors can't just show up in New York or Los Angeles and expect to break into the industry. They take acting classes first. They hone their craft. They build out their network and make contacts. Then, and only then, do they take the leap and try to start landing gigs. You might get lucky and be discovered on the streets of Los Angeles, but probably you won't. You need a plan if you want a reasonable chance of success.

The same is true of starting an organization or undertaking a mission. You need the right skills. You need the right knowledge. You need resources and the right team onboard. Most of all, you need a plan that sets out what skills and knowledge you need. You need to know what kind of team to assemble. That plan cannot be to just show up and hope for the best. That is a waste of everyone's time and resources.

Again, in concept, this is basic, common-sense stuff. And yet, every day, more and more people get in over their heads while trying to help, ultimately wasting the resources and time of everyone involved. This is especially true in nonprofit work, where people seem to think they don't need to be professionals. Wrong. Nonprofit organizations may not need to turn a profit like a business, but that doesn't mean they can be inefficient or ineffective. Ultimately, the money has to come from somewhere, whether it's your own pocket or a donor's. Either way, inefficiency wastes resources and capital that could go toward services and missions.

Efficiency is the result of pragmatic planning and preparation. Learn about what you are going to do. You wouldn't go into business without understanding your sector. Likewise, you shouldn't start an organization without knowledge of what you will be doing and whom you will be doing it for and with. Don't be like the hack writer who has never taken a writing class and tries to publish the first novel he ever writes. Don't be the wannabe actor who shows up in Hollywood without ever having taken an acting class. Don't be the failed businessperson who goes to market without a researched business plan. And, likewise, don't try to start an organization without understanding the basic functions and operation of an organization. If you want to lead an organization, you need to know how to communicate with donors, garner support, build and lead teams, execute missions, and more—all of that *in addition* to the area of expertise relevant to your operations and an understanding of the cause or community you are working with. Otherwise, you're sunk before you leave harbor.

There are plenty of ways to get the expertise you need. Reading this book is a good start, so that you can learn about what makes a movement successful, but you will need to do more. Learn about your mission and glean insights from the experts and those who came before. When starting a movement or organization, you are standing on the shoulders of giants. Take a look down. How did they do things? There is a wealth of information out there about how to do anything—and with the internet, it is all at your fingertips.

But there is also no substitute for hands-on experience doing the work and gaining familiarity with the people you are serving. If you want to work with a certain group of people, get to know those people. Want to fight addiction? Get out there and start talking to addicts so that you know what they need. Many people already know the population they are working with, which is why that is their passion. I know about veterans because I am one. Many people who work with addicts are former addicts themselves. But you don't have to be. You can join an organization like the one you want to start and learn the ropes before going out on your own to deliver a duplicate service in a different area, or perhaps deliver a needed service. But you'll never know what is needed, or who needs it, unless you get your hands dirty first and learn about what you want to do.

Next, develop the skills and area knowledge that you will need. You may have to learn some new things. I am always learning new things. Right now, I am brushing up on technology so that I can better reach out to younger veterans who grew up with social media. As a child of the 1980s, this is not something that comes naturally, but it is something I can learn, just as I learned about organizational structure, suicide prevention, veteran homelessness, and how to construct orphanages—none of which are things that I learned in my military career. When you want to educate yourself about something new, you can start by reading up on what you need to learn and then get hands-on experience by working with similar organizations. Again, you may already have many of the skills you need if you are working in your passion. I already knew how to lead humanitarian missions because, as a Special Ops officer in the military, I learned how to conduct missions in the field. The important thing is that you are aware of your knowledge gaps so that you can fill them.

Third, partner and recruit those with relevant skills. You don't have to do this all yourself, nor should you. You can contribute in certain areas while other people on your team do what you cannot. When I first started doing humanitarian missions, my role was security and logistics. I worked with a doctor who handled the medical services we were delivering. Neither of us could have carried out our missions alone, but together we were an unstoppable force for good. SOF Missions would have never gotten around to doing our first mission if I needed to finish medical school first. Doctors work with me because I have those skills. I work with them because they have medical expertise.

Pragmatism is simply the art and philosophy of coming prepared. You should understand every aspect of your operations, as well as the implication of your actions, *before* you start the mission. That is the only way to operate effectively and responsibly. Preparedness is everything and will determine your ultimate performance.

Sun Tzu, the legendary Chinese military strategist and philosopher, once wrote: "He will win who, prepared himself, waits to take the enemy unprepared." This always resonated with me as a military guy, but this is applicable to far more than warfare. His point is that you win or lose the battle not on the battlefield, but in the training field and while drawing up a strategy in the war room. This is as true in humanitarian work as it is on the battlefield. Your success will be determined by how prepared you are. Come prepared, or do everyone a favor and stay home. This may sound harsh, but you can actually do more harm than good by going into something unprepared. You can waste time and resources. In some cases, such as humanitarian missions in dangerous environments, you can even put lives at risk.

The hard truth is that many hear the call, few heed it, and fewer still succeed. If you are reading this book, there is a good chance you hear the call. You know that you want to change the world into a better place. You might even have a sense of exactly whom you want to help and how. In a sense, reading this book is the first small step toward heeding the call. Obviously, if you have not set out to start your organization, you are a long, long way from your goal, but everyone has to start somewhere.

But know this, regardless of how far you are in your undertaking, chances are, *statistically* speaking, the odds are stacked against you. That is because changing the world is hard and many movements fail to ignite. Countless organizations disband and go under, if they ever get off the ground in the first place. And a great deal of leaders never see their visions fully materialize.

That may sound discouraging, but it doesn't have to be. Come prepared, put in the work, stay the course, and results will follow. The reason most organizations fail has nothing to do chance. Many fail because their organizers and leaders did not properly prepare. They weren't pragmatic. They didn't learn about movement building. They didn't have a pragmatic plan for their vision. They just had a vision—and, maybe lots of hope, drive, and faith—but, as we now know, that's not enough.

It is not by chance that SOF Missions continues to grow and succeed. We started small, with a reasonable scope, doing humanitarian missions. My military background in Special Ops helped make that possible, as did the expertise of the medical professionals and contractors with whom I partnered. I also put in a lot of work to learn how to run an organization. No one just knows this stuff. You need to already have that skill set, having learned it on the job, or you need to put in the work to learn.

Many people know their purpose, and even have hope, drive, and faith, but they don't necessarily know how to be a good leader, articulate their ideology and mission, run an organization, develop and execute a strategy, or ignite a movement. Most people haven't studied movement theory, so they don't know what makes a movement successful. Most people haven't led a team or run an organization.

Coming into humanitarian work, I had a lot going for me. I already knew how to lead a team, strategize, operate in the field, devise a mission plan, and adjust on the fly. I learned much of that in the military, working in logistics and Special Operations, but I also learned a lot by working in the field, building on my knowledge with each new mission.

Still, I wish I knew then what I know now. It was only after operating SOF Missions for several years, albeit part-time while in the military and school, that I began to study movement theory and research historical movements. There is no need to reinvent the wheel when you can learn from those who came before you. Many great leaders have come before us, and we have the benefit of history to see what has worked and what has failed.

THE FOUR PILLARS OF MOVEMENT BUILDING

The entire purpose of this book is to provide a blueprint for building an organization that can ignite a movement. The information is gleaned from my dissertation, military experience, and nonprofit organization. I want to challenge you to change the world. I want to inspire you to do so. But most of all, I want to empower you with the knowledge so that you have a higher probability of making it happen. This book is meant to inspire would-be leaders to action, but it is first and foremost pragmatic. Good leaders are going to have hope, drive, and faith. What they won't necessarily have is the know-how to build a sound organization.

To that end, this book provides a simple model for movement building, what I call the Four Pillars, which is an amalgam of the entire history of movement theory rolled into a single model. You might be skeptical that one model can serve as a blueprint for all organizations. That is not my goal. Organizational structure is, in fact, only one pillar of the model. This is not just a model for building an organization, but for igniting an actual movement. An organization is just the formal, legal, and administrative structure that fuels the movement's mission. The actual movement is the people who get involved, including the leaders, the followers, the donors, the supporters, and those served. (Note that the same people often fill multiple roles, as with SOF Missions, which has veterans serving veterans.)

My main goal with this book is not just to help you build an organization, though that is part of my goal, because organizational structure is a key element in movement building. Later chapters of this book will discuss how to build an efficient, nimble, flexible, and resilient organization that can accomplish its mission. But I am not going to tell you how to achieve your mission. Instead, we are going to talk about why certain organizations have succeeded at igniting a movement and what they have in common.

These organizations all share certain traits that enable them to thrive and flourish. While every organization has its own strengths and specialties, successful organizations that have ignited movements share a predictable set of qualities. I call these commonalities "common critical factors," and while they do not encompass everything that a specific organization will need to tackle a specific problem, they do serve as a foundation that all organizations need to spark a movement.

The common critical factors align around these Four Pillars:

- Leadership
- Ideology
- Organizational Structure
- Strategy

The common critical factors are, in the aggregate, the lowest common denominators of successful movements. Implementing the common critical factors won't necessarily guarantee successful ignition of your movement, but as I have seen through experience they are extremely beneficial. They make up the Four Pillars that support an organization and its movement.

Think of the Four Pillars as a four-legged stool. Four legs are necessary for support. If one leg is missing or faulty, the stool will wobble or even collapse. This is no good for the movement, because the movement and mission are what sit on top of the stool, not the organization. The organization *is* the stool. The Four Pillars form the foundation for the organization that will allow it to ignite a movement—but only if they are working together to support the movement.

All four pillars must be addressed simultaneously and in concert or the movement will tumble and fail. Being exceptional at one pillar, or only certain factors, will not make up for deficiencies in another. The best leader in the world cannot ignite a movement with an incoherent ideology that isn't reflected in the organizational structure. The best-structured organization won't be able to launch a movement without an effective strategy for realizing the mission. Good leaders will find themselves stymied by an ineffective organization just as surely as a bad leader can tank a strong organization. You need all four pillars working together to support the movement. You have to engage all of the critical factors at once. The movement is only as strong as its weakest link.

The Four Pillars are not something I pulled out of thin air. Through my doctorate research, I saw the characteristics and consolidated them into four groups, which I named pillars. These pillars are generally agreed upon as key to movement building. I simply identified the common factors that were present in most movement theory models, whether they were formal or informal models, as well as actual historical movements, and arranged those factors around the pillars.

In my research, I looked at all the most successful movements throughout history, but with a special focus on Western culture, since I mostly work with organizations based in North America. (Many great movements have arisen from other cultures, of course, and the Four Pillars are universal enough to be applied anywhere. I simply focus on my own culture because that's where I am most effective.) Many of these movements look very different from the outside. They originally ignited from organizations from different historical eras and geographic locations. They involved different mission sets and operational scope. But what they had in common was their ability to inspire people and ignite a movement—and the Four Pillars, of course.

There is a reason that certain organizations or people are able to ignite movements and others are not. My aim with the Four Pillars is to succinctly explain what makes movements ignite so that more organizations can spark their own movement. I wanted to see if successful movements shared some spark and investigate it as a tool to build effective movements more efficiently. While the spark may or may not be "magic," or divine intervention it exists, and it can be mapped across the Four Pillars, a simple set of general concepts that serves as the tinder that ignites a movement.

The Four Pillars are certainly not magic. In a way, they are obvious. Movements are almost always started by *leaders* who are passionate about an *ideological cause* or mission for which they create an *organization* that can execute on a *strategy* as part of their mission. Leadership, ideology, organization, strategy: the Four Pillars, right there. Simple, right?

Wrong.

The Four Pillars are straightforward in concept, but the devil is always in the details. Of course, an organization needs competent leadership, a firm ideological grounding, proper organizational structure, and an effective strategy. Those are givens, almost no-brainers. But what does good leadership look like? How does one ensure that ideology not only guides the mission, but also informs the entire structure of the organization at every level? What is the best organizational structure? What makes certain strategies better than others?

The model and this book seek to answer questions like these. We will look to historical examples as our guide. No one will dispute that leadership is important, but many people spend their whole lives trying to become better leaders. By looking to those who came before and studying their movements, the model sets out not just to name the Four Pillars, but to define, quantify, and standardize them to create a template that can be used to replicate the success of other movements.

I want you to be able to use this model to actually build a movement. This model comes from the research conducted for my dissertation, but I am not interested in descriptive academic models. I am interested in creating an actionable tool for changing the world. This entire book, and the model contained therein, is a pragmatic tool to empower you to change the world. The Four Pillars are a blueprint for movement building. They show what does and doesn't work. They are based in a belief that pragmatism, preparedness, and expertise are necessary to ignite a movement.

In other words, you, as the leader, are going to have to do your homework. You have to roll up your sleeves and put in the hours. I don't just mean that you have to be willing to do the work, though you will have a lot of hard work ahead of you. But you also have to be willing to learn *how* to do the work. You need to learn best practices and follow them closely. You need to learn how to lead, how to build an organization, how to execute on a strategy, and how to ensure that the whole endeavor conforms to your ideology with consistency. You can't do any of that without learning about leadership and how nonprofits function. You can't do it without having thought long and hard about your ideology or how you will message and contextualize your work in a strategic manner to donors and those you want to serve. And you are setting yourself up to fail if you don't learn about other movements and what made them ignite.

Don't be the guy who goes in blind. Don't be the person who shows up unprepared and disappoints their followers and wastes everyone's time and money. Learn about leadership, ideological power, organizational structure, and strategic impact. Study the Four Pillars, understand the critical factors that ignite a movement, and learn how to apply them to your own mission to maximize your chances of success. Come prepared. Do the work.

This book can be the beginning of that work. These pages will *not* teach you everything you need to know about starting your specific organization. That would be beyond the scope of any one book. What this book *can* provide is a framework for setting up an organization that can ignite a movement. This book can't possibly teach you everything you need to know, but it should help you take off your blinders and see what you need to go out and learn. You need to know what you don't know to be able fill in the gaps in your knowledge.

That's just basic pragmatism—and you're going to need it in addition to your hope, drive, and faith.

So let's start talking about the elements of ignition.

CHAPTER 3

PILLAR I: THE HUMAN AGENT: HOW GOOD LEADERS ATTRACT COMMITTED FOLLOWERS

Movements are the sum of the followers who take up the cause. Without followers, without people, there is no movement. The people literally *are* the movement. There would be no movement without the human agent. However, not all human agents are equally influential. Leaders aren't the movement, but they are the spark that attract followers to the cause, which can ignite the movement.

There are, of course, different levels of leadership. Many people in the movement will be both leaders and followers. At SOF Missions, most people start out as followers by joining a team, but many go on to lead their own teams pursuing their own purpose within the parameters of SOF Missions' goal of empowering people to engage in God's mission—their ultimate purpose. These are leaders too, and will benefit from many of the traits we will discuss in this chapter. However, because this book is focused on *starting*, organizing, and igniting a movement, we will primarily be discussing leadership at the top operational level. The leaders discussed in this book are, for the most part, those who will continue to bear the torch of the movement.

Good leaders are neither born nor made—they are both. In my line of work, in both the military and in the humanitarian field, I see lots of people with the gifts of leadership. They are inspiring and motivating. They think outside the box. They have vision, not necessarily *a* vision yet, but they are visionary. These kinds of people are destined for success. They could make great movement leaders. But that doesn't mean they will actually do so. Many people with the right skills and traits for leadership go into business and either start companies or climb up the corporate ladder. They do very well for themselves in business.

Most people driven simply by money won't make it far in the nonprofit world. The hours are long and the compensation, most of the time, is far less. The movement has to be its own reward. I don't have millions of dollars, but I do have the satisfaction of knowing that the movement I helped create has now served eighty thousand people and counting. These people go on to serve other people who serve others. That's the kind of legacy I desire. I have never been driven by money, just a cause. I went into the military to *serve*. I took up humanitarian work to *serve*. And I founded SOF Missions to *serve* by empowering others to *serve* also. I believe that's God's plan for me: to *serve*.

Service has to be both your motivation and your reward. But what makes a person want to live a life of service? It might just begin with a flash point.

FLASH POINTS THAT SPARK MOVEMENTS

For many great leaders throughout history, the desire to lead is borne out of crisis or trauma. In his book *Movements That Change the World*, Steve Addison identifies "white-hot faith" as a flash point. This is a moment in time that flips an individual's world upside down. Many leaders come to a flash point through a great reckoning or crisis that tests—and ultimately confirms—their trajectory. People often turn to prayer when all else fails. When their prayers are answered, people often reevaluate their lives and seek out a higher purpose.

Of course, you don't have to be religious to have a flash point. Not everyone is religious, but all sentient, feeling humans are spiritual. Whether theist or atheist, people who undergo trial and surrender often question their lives. Many then surrender to a higher power and purpose, regardless of the nature of their spirituality. They forsake materialism in favor of that purpose. And the purpose they seek is from above. In my opinion, it's a God-driven purpose.

The hardship that brings many great leaders to a flash point is also what molds their vision. Very often, people start movements to help people facing the same problems that the movement leader faced. My own flash point came out of my struggles with posttraumatic stress, which made me passionate about veterans' issues. The hardships I faced as a Marine and an Air Force Special Ops officer were the genesis of SOF Missions. My flash point moment came in the Korengal Valley. While I struggled for years, the seventy-two hours of nonstop combat in the Valley of Death is what finally caused me to surrender to a higher power. We fought for three days straight just to survive and keep everyone on the team alive. Thankfully, we all survived. I returned home alive, but I came back as a changed man. I thought to myself, now what? I survived, but for what? The near-death experience exposed how meaningless my life really was. If I died in that valley, would it have really mattered? I wasn't sure, not based on the life I was living up until that point. I found myself regretting much of my entire life.

A recent study on regret, conducted by researchers at Cornell and the New School for Social Research, found that people regret what they *should* have done more than what they did wrong. In other words, we don't most regret failure—we most regret not trying at all. When faced with hardship, trauma, and especially death, people take stock of their lives. In these trying moments, we ask ourselves, "If I died today, would I be happy with the story of my life?" Hardship and struggle force us to face existential questions about regret and how we are spending our limited time on this earth.

For me, the answer was no. No, I was not living out my purpose. That is why I got into humanitarian work and recommitted myself to God and a life of service. Right there, I had my flash point. I began a new journey and thereafter devoted my life to what actually mattered. I wanted to live a life of purpose. I wanted to serve. I wanted to lead. I wanted my life to mean something.

This same story has played out all across history. Studying movement theory, I saw over and over again how many leaders came to their flashpoint through tragedy and hardship. Few people know that St. Patrick was kidnapped and enslaved by Irish pirates when he was only sixteen. The man who became the Apostle of Ireland wasn't even from Ireland. He was from Britain, but the pirates took him to Ireland and sold him into slavery. He went from being a privileged child of wealth to a slave overnight. For six years, he tended sheep for his master, a pagan priest of Druidism, before escaping with the help of British sailors. During his time in captivity, he became deeply religious and saw his enslavement as God's test of his faith. After returning home, he struggled with his ordeal. He suffered from what we might call trauma or PTSD today. His dreams were haunted by visions of pirates and warlords. But, rather than let that trauma destroy him, he channeled his energy into his faith. He went to France and studied to enter the priesthood. A vision came to him in which the poor pagan children of Ireland came to him holding out their empty hands. He was convinced that it was his mission to bring Christianity to Ireland and save these children. He returned to Ireland as a missionary to help the very people who kidnapped, enslaved, and abused him.

This same story continues today. Trauma and hardship are engendering white-hot faith in modern and contemporary leaders as well. Early in his career as a public speaker, Loren Cunningham, founder of Youth With A Mission, was traveling between speaking engagements when he got in a car accident. His wife was ejected from the vehicle. She lay in the road, limp and basically dead, and Loren asked for healing. Miraculously, she survived. Loren then doubled down on his mission to the movement he created.

In our work helping empower people to find and follow their own purpose with SOF Missions, I see white-hot faith up close and personal every day. One of our team leaders came to SOF Missions after having been injured in Afghanistan. He was an officer in the US Air Force. One night, the enemy started firing on his camp in the middle of the night. A stray shell tore through his cot and struck him in the back while he was sleeping. He suffered a spinal cord injury that left him a quadriplegic. He lost all feeling and use of the lower half of his body. He regained some function of the hands, but couldn't move his arms.

This was a traumatic experience in every way—physically, emotionally, and spiritually, he felt destroyed. Not only did he lose full use of his body, he also lost his identity as a warrior and breadwinner. He now depended on the wife and daughter who once depended on him. He couldn't support his family the way he wanted to. He could no longer serve his country. Feeling useless, he slipped into a deep depression.

"Now, what am I? Look at me," he said to me one day, gesturing with his head because he couldn't with his body.

He was daring me to say something. I choose my words carefully. While I struggled in my own life, my pain was nothing compared to his. I previously experienced PTSD-like symptoms. I nearly destroyed myself with self-destructive behavior. But I turned my life around and walked down a new path. This warrior would never be able to physically *walk* again. However, he could still walk a new path in a figurative sense.

"Let me ask you something, brother," I said. "How do you want your story to end? Do you want your whole story to be that you were an officer who got wounded and received a Purple Heart—and that's it, the end? Is that what you want? Because you're not dead, you got a second chance, and you still get to choose how your story ends."

While his injury would always affect him—there was no way around that—it did not have to define him. He got to tell the story of his life, not the injury. He could still find hope, joy, and happiness. He could still change the world. But he took control of his story. His story could be one of tragedy—or it could be one of *inspiration*. I knew this to be true because every day at SOF Missions we see the hurt and wounded persevere and inspire others.

"God has a radical calling in your life. Find your ultimate purpose and show the world what you can do," I told him. "Show them what *they* can do."

This warrior went on to join SOF Missions. He eventually created SOF teams of his own, which focus on adaptive physical training. He works with people who have spinal cord injuries, many of them veterans, though the program is open to everyone. Because unfortunately there is a high demand for this kind of work, we split the first team into two support groups. Now, he is changing lives every day. He is also an advisor on military affairs to a US congressman. He's happy and fulfilled, successful, a real leader. He is a poster child for white-hot faith. He took his trauma and tragedy and, rather than let them destroy him, built a life of service fighting against hardship. He is a true inspiration. And he did it by telling his own story rather than having it dictated to him. He refused to be a statistic or a charity case and chose to be an inspiration instead.

If you want to lead, you have to do the same. What's your story going to be? We all face hardship, but we don't have to let it define us. There are seven billion other people on this planet, each of us unique, with our own story and testimony. While each story is unique, your story will resonate with others facing the same trials and tribulations. Those people are potential followers. They are your movement. You just have to inspire them to follow.

How will you inspire them? You can't just put out a sob story and hope to inspire people. You need to have a vision and be able to communicate it to others. That is something that makes leaders great. And there is a specific set of leadership traits that represents one of the pillars of igniting a movement. Many of the great leaders who have ignited movements shared most of these traits.

And you can share them too. You may already possess some. You may have to work at others. But remember, great leaders are born and made. You can hone and develop, or even compensate for, traits you do not already possess.

By studying the leaders of historical movements and contemporary humanitarian organizations, I have isolated the traits most strongly correlated to good leadership. We will discuss some of these traits more than others, as some are straightforward, whereas others are counterintuitive. Also, some traits are more strongly correlated with good leadership; therefore, we will give them special attention. Finally, some are so central to igniting a movement that they demand thorough discussion.

The traits most strongly correlated with leadership among people who have ignited movements include:

- Passion
- Perseverance
- Experience
- Modeling
- Vision
- Strategic thinking
- Humility

Let's look at these traits more closely.

PASSION

Passion is what drives people to lead. Great leaders are often driven by a powerful and sometimes controllable sense of passion. This can be a powerful source of energy and inspiration. As we discussed in the first chapter, your mission should reflect your true purpose. Most people who experience a flash point and go on to answer their call and find their purpose know exactly what they are passionate about and what they want to accomplish. If you're reading this book, you probably already have a cause in mind, if not a specific mission. The great movement leaders throughout history were all driven by passion for a specific cause, usually something that radically changed their own life.

Passion is important because it is what sustains your hope, drive, and faith. Passion for the mission translates into passion for the work. It is one thing to simply want a better world, and a whole other thing to want to do the work of making the world better. Having passion for the cause keeps you motivated, your team inspired and productive, and contributes to perseverance. I would not be able to sustain my work with SOF Missions if I weren't passionate about veterans and mission work.

While every movement has its own causes, most leaders are also passionate about vital principles, such as freedom, liberty, and the easing of suffering and oppression. Many humanitarian leaders get into this business to improve individual lives and the world at large. Movement leaders tend to not only be passionate about the cause, but also passionate about altruism and justice. Great leaders who create meaningful movements all want to make the world better. If you're in this for fortune or fame, you're going to be sorely disappointed.

It really has to be passion, not money, that drives you. I can think of a few shady televangelists and hucksters who run organizations for a profit, but none of them have actually ignited movements. Their organizations tend to die with them.

PERSEVERANCE

No one can spearhead a movement without grit and determination in the face of adversity. Igniting a movement takes time and energy in great and equal measure. Things are sometimes going to be difficult. If you're going to quit when it gets hard, your chances of success diminish drastically. I have always prescribed to the "all in" approach. That way, when times are tough, you'll have the right attitude to overcome. Without the right attitude, it's best to wait until you are ready.

Perseverance is a potent weapon. When I was a kid raised in the violent streets of Los Angeles, I persevered. When my biological father told me, I wouldn't make it without him, I persevered. When I had a dream to go to college and my teacher told me I wasn't smart enough, I persevered. When I started running for a future and people told me I couldn't compete at the national level, I preserved. When I applied to the Marine Corps and people told me I couldn't get through boot camp, I preserved. When I assessed for the elite operations and peers told me I couldn't make, I persevered. When I was surrounded by an overwhelming enemy in the mountains of Afghanistan, I persevered. Perseverance has been by my side against every conflict in my life and it has served me well.

Perseverance, as we explained earlier, is derived from your hope, drive, and faith. These represent the foundation of *sustainable* leadership that can stand the test of time and hardships. To sustain an ignition, you must persevere.

EXPERIENCE

Experience is correlated with good leadership, but less so than you might think. The important thing is to have *relevant* experience. You don't necessarily need to have a doctorate or decades of experience, but you do need to know about the people you are trying to help. You should be knowledgeable about the area you are trying to serve. If you want to help house the homeless population in your local community, become familiar with the homeless community. Get out there, shake hands, talk to people, and find out what they actually need. Learn about the relevant laws and policies. Time is extremely valuable, so don't waste it.

For example, most people wouldn't know that New York City has laws that *require* the city to provide housing to everyone. The problem isn't a lack of shelters. The problem is that many homeless people choose not to use the shelters, often due to drug and alcohol problems or mental health issues. Some professionals would say that you are wasting your time advocating for more shelters when the community actually needs better access to mental health services and addiction treatment.

You shouldn't feel hampered by your current experience level and skill set. You can always go out and learn more by studying and doing. Invest in yourself and gain the experience and skills you need to lead the mission. You don't necessarily need formal training. Education can help, but don't let it be a barrier to pursuing your mission or getting the experience you want or need. Training and education can be a starting point, but experience is ultimately about getting your hands dirty.

You don't have to do everything yourself, which means you don't need to be able to do everything yourself. Movements are, by definition, made up of many people all contributing. You can delegate. When the movement grows to a certain size, you need to delegate. If you don't have all of the relevant experience you need, go partner with other organizations and individuals. Find partners with the skills you need. Working together not only gets more things done, but it can bolster your knowledge base.

MODELING

The old adage is true: actions speak louder than words. While interviewing leaders in the nonprofit and mission fields, we found many of them agreed that good leaders were good role models. They don't just talk the talk—they walk the walk too. They lead by example.

There is no more powerful way of conveying your vision than living it out in your own life. At SOF Missions, we believe in the radical power of service. Veterans see our team serving others, meeting them where they are, not being judgmental, and dedicating ourselves to a higher purpose. When they see others acting with compassion and purpose, they are compelled to do the same. When they literally *see* how service can transform lives, they want to serve. Nothing—no slogan, pamphlet, or ad campaign—could ever so effectively convey our vision.

For my money, there has never been a greater movement leader than Jesus. And he was empowered to live out his principles. He did not merely say that we should feed and share with the poor. He did so. His life was a life of service, not just talking about service. He lived by the principles he was trying to impart, and he encouraged others to emulate his behavior—and they did so in droves. In the book Acts, the author, Luke, who was a Greek physician, writes that the followers of Jesus are turning the world upside down. Here we are, two thousand years later, and Christianity is the world's largest religion with more than two billion followers.

None of us are Jesus—we are just mortals—but we can follow his example and, well, lead by example.

VISION

Leading a movement is not about managing people. It will be hard to garner followers unless you inspire them with a clear vision. You have to communicate your vision in a way that motivates people to get involved. Building movements is all about inspiring people to take up the cause. Your followers need to be excited about the vision, which is why the greatest movement leaders have all been great visionaries.

This has been true across all of history and remains true today. The people who ignite great movements are people of great vision. They are dreamers. They're big thinkers. They have grand, ambitious, even radical ideas. I've spoken to scores of people at the top of the humanitarian field. They all list vision as one of the primary traits of effective leaders.

This makes intuitive sense. After all, what is a movement but a vision put into action by many people? Founders, by definition, need to be visionary, because without a vision there is no movement. Movements are made up of inspired people. What inspires them? The vision. That vision is usually just a plan to execute on a cause. Visionary leaders are good at coming up with creative ways to address big problems.

Vision is *not* intelligence or even a function of intelligence. Surprisingly, intelligence is not highly correlated with good leadership. Of course, most people who found successful organizations are fairly intelligent, but being a genius does not make you more likely to ignite a movement. A high IQ is not predictive of success. Vision is predictive of success because it comes from inspiration, and the way to get people to join a movement is by inspiring them. People aren't inspired by intellectual, complex ideas. They're inspired by creative, singular ideas that speak to a purpose and address a problem. You don't have to be the most intelligent person in the room to have the best idea. You just have to be inspired and know something about the problem you want to solve and the people you want to help. I am rarely the smartest guy in the room, but I am a big thinker.

STRATEGIC THINKING

Of course, there's more to executing on an idea than simply having a vision. The vision is just the dream. It will stay a dream unless you put it into action. Leaders can't just be dreamers. They have to eventually come back down to earth and think strategically about how to make the dream a reality. Any person can crank out big ideas, but great leaders analyze, vet, critique, and workshop their ideas into something practical and actionable.

This is a matter of pragmatism; figuring out how to implement your vision. My vision for SOF Missions was to help veterans find healing and discover their purpose through service to others. Sounds like a good plan, right? But it's not a plan. It's a vision. To make that vision a reality we came up with an actual program and plan that could be implemented on the ground—and that requires strategic thinking.

Vision is the concept. Strategic thinking is the implementation. We are not talking ground-level tactics but rather the big moving parts of how an organization implements an idea. After my epiphany while out on a humanitarian mission in Peru, where SOF Missions changed direction toward a primary focus on healing veterans, we figured out how we were going to accomplish this mission. We decided how new SOF teams would be formed and managed. We designed a program that addressed the whole warrior: mentally, physically, and spiritually. We developed a three-step holistic healing model that was unique. Going into this, I knew I wanted to empower people so they could be a part of changing the world for the common good; now the focus narrowed to helping veterans find hope. In the process, we could harness the power of service to empower and heal veterans. That was the whole vision, period. But to make SOF Missions as it exists today a reality, I sat down and thought strategically about the vision.

You don't necessarily have to do this alone. Good leaders rely on counsel and advice. I think of myself as a visionary thinker. I'm also a solid tactician, thanks to skills I picked up in Special Operations, but strategy isn't always my strongest suit. I am not always the most pragmatic thinker. My wife is much more of a pragmatic thinker. When I come to her with my new, great, big idea, she helps me flesh out my vision. She reins me in and brings me back down to earth. She will break out a pen and paper and start jotting things down. She asks questions. She helps me find the weak points and possible challenges. Together, as the founders of SOF Missions, we hammer out the fine details.

Without strategic thinking, there is no way to communicate your vision to others. Humans are not telepathic. No one can enter your head and see your vision. It's critical you are able to articulate the vision to others. There's no way to do that without getting down into the details of how a project, mission, or organization will actually carry out the vision.

HUMILITY

When we think of strong leaders throughout history, humility is not the first trait that comes to mind. However, in my research humility is the number one trait most correlated with good leadership. This may come as a surprise—it did for me while conducting my research. We think of great leaders as bold, commanding figures with type A personalities. They are headstrong and fearless in the face of adversity. But are they humble?

The answer is yes. They should be both strong *and* humble.

In his groundbreaking book, *Good to Great*, Jim Collins notes that great leadership is "a study in duality: modest and willful, humble and fearless." Collins contends that great business leaders don't talk about themselves, but rather their companies and the contributions of others. They are firm and commanding, sure-footed, and able to act under pressure—but they are also deeply humble. They respect the contributions of their teams.

Though Collins was speaking of the private sector, his observation on "Level 5 good-to-great leaders," as he calls them, can apply to nonprofits and movements as well. In fact, I would say humility is even *more* important in the nonprofit world. Many nonprofit organizations, especially when starting out, rely on volunteers. These people are giving their time and energy for free. If you, as the leader, don't respect and acknowledge that contribution, they will probably stop showing up. Even those in paid staff positions tend to make less than they could in the private sector. They will quit if you don't treat them well and acknowledge that their collective contribution to the movement is far greater than your own personal contribution as the leader.

The same is true of donors and board members. They are lending their time, expertise, or name to the cause. SOF Missions is supported by lots of people. They aren't doing it for the money. They *give* money. They *give* resources. They *give* time. Each is critical to the success of the organization. They help us network and make connections. I am humbled by their generosity and take none of it for granted—not the money, resources, time, nor any form of support.

Humility is not only important to the ignition of a movement, but also to an organization's long-term success. In my experience, there are two kinds of leaders: humble leaders and tyrannical leaders. The latter have a hard time keeping an organization together.

This is because tyrannical leaders rule by decree. They call the shots with little input from others. They don't listen to others and they don't play well on a team. Everything is their way or the highway. This is an ineffective way to lead. No one, no matter how brilliant, is always right. No one should be running an organization as if they know everything. Tyrannical leaders are often hesitant to admit when they are wrong. They get so caught up in their own egos that they stay the course on a failed strategy or policy rather than admit that they made a mistake. They are not only more likely to make bad decisions, because they don't accept counsel, but also to stay the course when things aren't going well.

Humble leaders don't let their ego get in the way of making good decisions. They don't just decree. They communicate, which is a two-way street. Good leaders don't just talk, they also *listen*. They take counsel. They are receptive to feedback. Their positions are more effective because they are informed by many points of view and draw upon the collective insight of the many. Humble leaders surround themselves with other smart and inspired people, not just yes men, and take other people's advice to heart. They work collectively as a team and do not always have to be the center of attention. They make decisions that are good for the movement, not themselves. They trust, value, and center the input of others.

All of my heroes were humble leaders. Franklin Graham, who headed Samaritan's Purse, is known for being especially receptive to input. He doesn't have to be the guy with the answer. He surrounds himself with smart people and listens to the counsel of others. Ultimately, he makes the major executive decisions, but he does so with the insight and input of others. Loren Cunningham, of Youth With A Mission, is known for the same way. He implemented a strategic plan that involved his "Seven Global Leaders" who would each represent their area of the world. Each contribute evenly to the movement. The structure allowed the movement to be as effective as possible. I model myself after these kinds of leaders. At SOF Missions, I surround myself with super-smart people and listen to their input.

I wasn't always this way though. During my first humanitarian mission to the Amazon, I got into an argument with someone from the host organization. I was running operations and was very focused on security. I wanted everyone coming into the clinic enter through a funnel so that we could control the flow of traffic. This is a basic security protocol when operating in Iraq and Afghanistan, but the leader of the host organization believed it was unnecessary and would offend the local community. She was adamant about doing things her way, but so was I. She knew more about the local community, but I knew more about security. Unfortunately, I refused to even consider her input.

"Look, I am in charge of security," I said. "It's my way, or we're not doing it."

This caused a lot of tension, both between our teams and also within my own team. They rightfully blamed the tension on me. I was not being diplomatic or appreciative. There was no reason to be so headstrong, especially in an area that was low threat. I was being tyrannical and unbending. It was only after reflection that I realized the error of my ways. We were on the mission together. We all had skills and knowledge. I was the security expert, but she was the expert on this community, and we both had something to contribute. But being so inflexible kept us from actually working together effectively. The mission was about bringing hope, distributing medicine, and providing care, not about doing things my way.

I set my ego aside and apologized. I listened carefully to what she was saying and tried to really value her input. We talked for an hour straight. I listened to her concerns, and only then did I explain my concerns. And, guess what? In the end, we came to a compromise solution that would be the least disruptive and that wouldn't offend the village elders. We came to a decision that satisfied our concerns, mine included, and it only happened because I was humble, attentive, and verbally appreciative. Everything went according to plan and everyone was happy. But it only worked once I stopped trying to be an autocratic leader and instead practiced humility. This was a life lesson on many levels.

Remaining humble is an active and ongoing process. Visionary leaders are often headstrong. Founders tend to have Type A personalities, which is great for getting things done and taking the lead, but can also lead to counterproductive behavior if unchecked. You want to be confident, not cocky, arrogant, pompous, or narcissistic. This kind of behavior destroys morale and can tear a mission, team, or entire organization apart.

While tyrannical leaders and humble leaders can both get an organization off the ground, only humble leaders are able to sustain a movement. Autocratic leaders eventually wear out their followers. You can only push people around so much until they become tired, frustrated, and exhausted. No matter how much they care about the cause, they will abandon the movement if they don't think you care about them. You have to be humble and appreciative.

Humble leaders create a self-sustaining movement that new leaders and followers will want to join. Humble leaders are always thinking about their successors. Why? Because it's not about them— it's about a cause. They create organizations that don't require them to be present to crack the whip and lead like an autocrat. Many of the great movements in history continue to live on well past the demise or departure of the original leader. Samaritan's Purse, Youth With A Mission, Overseas Mission Fellowship (formerly known as China Inland Mission)—these movements all still exist today. They are hammering away at the same cause, just under new leadership.

HOW TO INSPIRE FOLLOWERS

The leadership traits discussed here are effective because they will help you lead. They will also help you attract followers to the movement. Movements need followers. The job of the leader is to motivate and mobilize followers. At the most basic level, that is how you build a movement. You have to motivate people to take action. And you can only do that by inspiring them.

Great leaders empower their followers and show them how to make a difference. While natural leaders are often intrinsically motivated, many people lack drive and motivation because they don't think they can make a real difference. Good leaders empower people to act by showing them how they can make a difference. They guide and mentor followers, showing them exactly how and where they can make an impact and inspiring them to do so.

People join movements to be a part of something bigger and greater than themselves. They won't join your movement unless it inspires them and they believe it can affect real change. To be inspirational, then, you cannot just be a visionary—you also need to be an effective leader with an effective organization, strategy, and vision. In other words, the Four Pillars of movement ignition are required to attract followers and keep them inspired. Without the Four Pillars in place, you will struggle to keep followers. They have to feel supported by the *organization* and trust the *strategy*. The *ideology* has to resonate with them. And they have to be inspired by you, the *leader*.

A strong leader isn't enough—movements need all four legs—but the human agent is special because it is *you*, the leader who inspires a population. Ultimately, it is up to you to make sure that the Four Pillars are implemented effectively.

Those traits are critical to attract followers and instill confidence in you and the movement. Having passion, experience, and perseverance shows followers that you know what you are doing, that you care, and that you won't bail on the movement. Being a good model for the principles of the movement shows that you are an authentic leader. Having vision and being able to communicate it effectively allow you to inspire people. Humility keeps you from driving people away with arrogance or silencing their voices. Followers want to know that their leaders are human and fallible.

None of this can be faked, not over the long haul. The most inspiring leaders are authentic. They are genuine in their actions and sincere in their commitment to the mission. You have to show people that you are genuine. You are asking them to give their time, energy, and resources to a movement. If you don't truly believe in the cause, why should they?

CHAPTER 4

PILLAR II: IDEOLOGY: THE SHARED CONVICTIONS THAT UNITE A MOVEMENT

Movements are made up of people driven by a shared ideology. Movements can't exist without a coherent driving ideology. Ideology is one of the Four Pillars and a prerequisite to movement ignition. A movement without ideology is just a gathering of random people with no sense of shared purpose. That's not what movements are. Movements are a body of people rallying behind a singular vision.

Movement participants share the same vision because of their shared ideology. Successful movements need to be ideologically cohesive by definition. We only pursue causes that align with our fundamental understanding of the world and our core values. No one is going to join a movement founded on ideological principles that don't match their own—or at least those that they would be willing to adopt.

Many people come into contact with SOF Missions as secularists or atheists but then realize the word of God speaks to them when they find healing through it. But these people were willing to accept God's teachings. They were amenable to the ideology.

People who subscribe to your ideology, or who are amenable to it, are your potential followers. I would like to think that everyone wants a better world, and many of us are working toward one. But different movements have different visions of a better world. They focus on different priorities. We are all fighting for a better world, but how we conceive of a better world is a function of our ideology. Your movement has to be built around people who share your vision of a better world.

Ideology is the system of beliefs that guides the movement and dictates the mission. Christian missionaries go overseas to teach people about Jesus because they are driven by Christ's command in the bible to share its message. They encourage others to join in, learn more about God, and ultimately themselves share the message with others. This sense of purpose wouldn't even exist without the Christian ideology.

Ideology is the basic foundation shared by all the members of a movement. The movement actually emerges from the ideology, not the other way around. Leaders don't dictate the ideology. They simply undertake a mission, based on their own ideology, and are followed by those who share their beliefs. Their ideology is what attracts them to the cause. Ideology is why they care. It is why they act. If the mission is the *what*, then the ideology is the *why*.

No shared ideology, no shared mission. No shared mission, no movement.

Everyone has an ideology. We all have beliefs and core principles that guide our values. I am not here to give you an ideology. You already have one. Instead, I want to introduce you to the ideological practices that have helped organizations spark movements. You have an ideology, but it may not be well articulated and centered in your daily life. Organizations that adopt a mission and practices around a cohesive ideology are far more likely to ignite and sustain movements.

In fact, virtually all successful movements share these ideological factors and practices:

- adherence to a written ideological guidebook,

- a common ideological spirit shared by the movement,

- practices of spiritual formation that reinforce and crystalize the ideology,

- ideological commitment, and/or

- rest and recuperation time dedicated to ideological reflection.

Let's consider each of these in turn.

THE GUIDEBOOK

Ideologies don't just spring up from nowhere. Most ideologies are derived from longstanding spiritual traditions and thought that stretch far back into history. Ideologies are codified by texts, which serve as ideological guidebooks. This is the manual that the movement refers to when developing strategies, operations, tactics, and all other practices. These actions should reflect the ideology and can be referenced to make sure the movement is staying on course.

For me, as a Christian, my guidebook is the Bible. It is my ideological foundation and also serves as my playbook. Depending on the situation, it can provide tactics and strategies that can be deployed to further the mission. For these tactics and strategies to help others, those people need to be ideologically compatible with the source text. Not everyone working with SOF Missions is Christian, but we do ask that all staff members respect our ideological position. While we serve all veterans, not just Christians, we do explain that SOF Missions takes a biblical approach with all of our programs and services. We believe in the power of God and that he can change and transform any life. When we try to change lives, we do so by helping people embrace God. That is who we are and what we do.

What we have found is that SOF Missions is most appealing, and most helpful, to those who share our core values, even if they are not practicing Christians. Many people, after going through the program and joining an SOF team, which is simply a "group with a purpose" within the movement, become people of faith in the process. That's a personal decision they make—we don't force that on them—but that so many make that choice when they see the healing power of God shows that they were amendable to the ideology all along.

The Bible is not the only ideological guidebook at your disposal. There are also more secular documents that can help establish your ideology, some of which are even important to me and SOF Missions. For me, the founding documents of our nation fall into this category. Like most veterans, I am extremely patriotic. As soldiers, we put country before ourselves, just as we put God before ourselves. Most veterans view the US Constitution as something worth fighting and dying for—many actually have. Thus, the Constitution, the Declaration of Independence, and our other founding documents can also serve as a source text that establishes your deeply held ideological convictions. These texts form the ideological basis for our nation and are rooted in deep ideals about how we as Americans should live. I will always put God's law over man's law, but I also still find the

Constitution to be an almost sacred text that informs my values and ideology.

Some organizations write their own texts that clarify ideological principles and how they fit into the mission. These texts are sometimes influenced by other traditional ideological texts that are extracted from the guidebook. Alcoholics Anonymous has the *Big Book*, which is based in Judeo-Christian theism, to guide members. *The Foundational Values of Youth With A Mission*, a text produced by Youth With A Mission, describes the movement's guiding principles and values that the members "hold in high regard, which determine who we are, how we live, and how we make decisions." These self-produced ideological texts can help to clarify the guidebook, but it is important to understand that they aren't the source of the ideological guidebook. Both of these organizations are based in Christian doctrine and didn't just make up their ideology. Ideologies are not usually the movement leader's creation. Movement leaders follow an established ideology.

Whatever your ideology, secular or religious, find the texts that inform your ideology and let them be your guide. Your ideology should be built on a long tradition of thought. Find the source texts that reflect your deep ideological foundation. Read them daily. Encourage your followers to do the same. Use them as a yardstick or level to keep your movement centered around its ideological core.

ESPRIT DE CORPS

In the Marine Corps, we would split into four-man squads for tactical operations, called fire teams. Once we were in gear and moving, we were excited. We were on fire. We were ready to take on the objective and complete the mission. And we were all on fire *together*—we fed off of each other's spirit.

That shared spirit is *esprit de corps*, which means spirit of the body, as in a body of people. What is a movement but a body of people with a shared spirit? That *defines* a movement. Esprit de corps is the shared spirit of the movement members that inspires participation, enthusiasm, devotion, and kinship within the movement.

This shared spirit creates a deep bond among movement members. Author and theologian Howard Snyder claimed healthy movements are "conscious of being a distinct covenant-based community." He was speaking specifically of renewal movements, which attempt to revitalize the church for the modern age, but his words apply to all movements. Movements are based around a commitment to the cause and the rest of the movement. They go hand in hand. When you fight together, on ideological grounds, you function as one. The burning commitment to the cause creates deep commitment to others who are part of the movement.

In the Marine Corps, and within all of the branches of the military, we make a commitment to die for our fellow brothers in arms. We are so ideologically committed to the cause that we are committed to the group as well. Marines will live and die for the cause of freedom and country. When I go into combat with my brothers, we operate as one entity. We go in knowing that we will take a bullet for someone else. We operate as one *body*. The distinction between me and them becomes almost meaningless. We have entered a covenant to serve the mission and protect each other.

Most successful movements in history have been covenant based. Throughout history, the majority of successful movements have been spearheaded by people of faith. They understand the sanctity of a covenant and are familiar with living under a shared ideology. The word "covenant" is derived from the Latin phrase *con venire*, meaning a coming together, and that is what a movement is. Movements are a coming together of people, fueled by a shared esprit de corps, to make change in the world.

The covenant is no joke. This is a serious commitment of togetherness. One of my favorite historical movements is that of the Jesuits, who in 1540 formed the Society of Jesus, a scholarly Christian congregation that centered its ideology in an evangelical missionary movement. As part of their covenant with the movement, the Jesuits agreed to take the mission anywhere, often requiring them to be dispatched to places where they were subjected to extreme and unsafe living conditions. This was a covenant if ever there was one. They came together to form a movement that, according to their founding documents, was founded for "whoever desires to serve as a soldier of God, to strive especially for the defense and propagation of the faith and for the progress of souls in Christian life and *doctrine.*" They made a commitment to the ideology and also to one another to pursue their mission. They considered themselves soldiers of God and throughout history have sometimes been called "the Company." Their faith and ideology have helped bind the movement together for almost five hundred years.

Your organization doesn't have to span continents and centuries to succeed, but you can learn something about movement building by taking a page from the Jesuits and the bond and sense of devotion forged by their shared ideological commitment.

SPIRITUAL FORMATION

Ideologies lay out the ideas and principles of a movement, but they aren't just words on paper. They exist in our hearts and minds and get expressed in the real world through our actions and practices. These practices are active manifestations of the ideology. Without them, the ideology isn't *real.* These deeply held convictions aren't deeply held unless they actually inform our behavior. Ideology isn't a passive thing you carry around; it has to be lived out and practiced. True, deeply felt ideology manifests itself in how you live your life and go about your day. In other words, you can't just talk the talk, you have to walk the walk too.

Ideology is not just the beliefs, but also the practices that arise from those beliefs. Protestantism gives us a name for these practices and behaviors. We call them *spiritual formation*, a useful term in movement theory regardless of your ideological foundation. Spiritual formation refers to the processes and practices that are informed by ideology. These practices, which allow people to live out their ideology, can include prayer and meditation, spiritual disciplines, and other ways of expressing commitment to and reflection upon ideology.

Spiritual formation is pragmatic. Spiritual formation keeps people connected to the movement's cause. This is an active *practice*, one performed consistently, often every day. Whatever your ideology, spiritual formation means really living that ideology and centering it in your life and in the movement. In my case, as someone whose personal ideology is rooted in Christian doctrine, I have to actually live as the Bible intends and make it part of my everyday life.

Unfortunately, not all self-professed Christians actually live this way. The Public Religion Research Institute issued a report in 2017 showing that about two-thirds of Americans identify as some kind of Christian. That translates into roughly one hundred million Christian Americans. Now, while I would never question someone's religious or spiritual convictions, we all know for a fact that not all self-identified Christians actually center their lives around God. Not all Christians are truly ideologically driven by Christian doctrine. Lots of people identify as Christian, sometimes culturally, but also religiously, without really living and breathing the Christian ideology. They don't allow the word of God to manifest in their daily actions and practices.

This isn't a critique. It's just a sad truth. I don't go around criticizing how people practice their faith or spirituality. However, this kind of "one-foot-in, one-foot-out" approach to Christianity is not a strong ideological foundation for a movement. For a movement to ignite, the members share an ideology and are fully committed to it. They engage in practices that reflect that ideology in their lives and the movement. These practices make the ideology real and present. They keep the movement cohesive and on track.

If your movement is going to be based on Christian ideology, or any ideology, you need to implement practices that reflect and reinforce that ideology. At SOF Missions, we operate under an ideology that centers Christ and advocates for getting to know God and serving Him and our fellow man. At my core, I truly believe that the secret to creating a better life and a better world is to live like Jesus by loving God, loving your fellow man, and following the Golden Rule of doing unto others as you would have them do unto you. I literally live my life by the example set out by Jesus. I adopt practices that reflect this belief. In doing so, I am not just claiming an ideology—I'm actually *living* my ideology, both in my personal life and in the work I do with SOF Missions.

That's a whole lot more meaningful and powerful than just claiming to be a Christian, which means little unless you are committed to Christian doctrine and live out Biblical principles in your life. Just saying you're a Christian isn't enough to get other people who are driven by Christian ideology to follow you and your movement. The ideology informs your practices as much as it informs theirs.

This extends beyond matters strictly of faith. Many armchair "humanitarians" and social media "activists" post about causes online but don't do much to advance those causes in the real world. This does not reflect a real commitment to service or an ideological purpose. In my humble opinion, you are never going to inspire followers by sharing memes or voicing opinions on social media.

What does inspire people is seeing someone passionately moved to act upon their ideology. If you want to ignite a movement, you have to live your ideology, not just post about it on Facebook. Real humanitarians are actively engaged; many travel the world and fight for justice, equality, liberty, and freedom from oppression. They go out and *do* things. They don't just *talk* about rendering aid—they actually render it.

Just think—what if I had the audacity to write this book without actually being a humanitarian who conducts movements and organizes people? You probably wouldn't care about what I had to say about movement building. And you'd be right not to care. Words don't give actions credibility. Actions give words credibility.

Practices of spiritual formation aren't passive. They are *acts* and real-world expressions of ideology. Deep reflection is a very active pursuit that keeps the movement centered on its ideology. Adopting practices like prayer and meditation will keep you on course. Integrate them into your daily routine. Have your followers do the same. They will keep everyone connected with each other and the cause, reinforcing the esprit de corps and strengthening the movement.

The relationship between ideological beliefs and practices of spiritual formation is cyclical. The beliefs inform the practices, and the practices reinforce the beliefs. This is why organizations that engage in spiritual formation practices are so much more likely to ignite a movement. These practices bring the movement together and remind everyone why they took up the cause.

If you don't stay focused on the ideology on a daily basis, you can easily lose track of why you undertook the mission. Many organizations fail or fizzle out over time as they lose their sense of purpose. Running an organization is hard. Volunteering is hard. Working in nonprofits can be exhausting. Burnout and the daily grind are real. If the movement is not established on a strong ideological foundation that manifests itself in daily practices, people start to forget why they joined. Cynicism and burnout can set in. It is easy to lose sight of the purpose entirely. Eventually, people lose interest or hope, and the movement begins to collapse.

Practices of spiritual formation help movements stay on track and help prevent this fate. Spiritual practices reinforce the ideology, which helps ensure that the mission and operations reflect the ideology. If the mission is the *what*, then the ideology is the *why*. If you don't know why you are doing something, you'll soon start to question the endeavor—and rightfully so! The practices of spiritual formation keep you ideologically centered.

While practices are mission-critical to igniting a movement, they can be simple things. They are daily rituals and small actions that keep the focus on the *why* so that you don't veer off course with the *what*. The most common practices of spiritual formation are simply prayer, meditation, and active and communal ideological reflection on what you are doing in the moment.

Prayer and meditation are very similar. Both require you to focus on things closely and to the exclusion of other matters. They both require you to empty your mind and experience a "death to self", in which your own existence falls away and you can see things more clearly. With prayer, I do this by speaking directly to God about a matter. While meditating, which I also do regularly, I speak to my inner self, my spirit, my soul. Prayer and meditation end up being functionally similar. Both allow me to remove myself from the equation until the only thing left is the inner ideology that guides me, allowing me to solve problems and overcome obstacles in ways that align with my ideology. Try both and see what works for you.

The research I conducted noted that these practices are necessary for movement building. The same ideology that drives leaders also drives followers. They too need to participate in daily reminders that their work matters. While researching movements and nonprofit organizations, I found that the most successful nonprofit organizations were those that gathered daily for prayer. This is not just the power of answered prayers, but also the power of spiritual formation. Time and time again, I observed that organizations that succeeded in igniting movements came together to pray for the cause on a regular basis. They each fought for a different cause, but they all gathered together for prayer. This designated time for prayer allowed the movement to come together and focus on what they were doing and why. The practice sharpened their ideological sense of purpose and fostered a community spirit.

There is no better example of the power of spiritual formation than the Moravians, a Christian sect that peeled away from the Catholic Church a full century before the Protestant Reformation. There was a major Moravian revival in the eighteenth century, and the sect became the first non-Catholic church to do missionary work, which they were very good at. They established some thirty settlements and sent hundreds of missionaries out into the world. Suddenly, the Moravians ignited a powerful worldwide movement. They were known for their ideological commitment, which they practiced through prayer. They conducted the first continuous prayer vigil, which continued for twenty-four hours a day, day and night, for more than *a hundred years.*

Now, a hundred-year vigil is perhaps the most extreme form of daily practices, but it worked for the Moravians. You don't have to conduct spiritual formation nonstop for the rest of your life, but your movement should incorporate these kinds of practices into your day. Many contemporary organizations practice daily prayer or moments of silence for reflection. Everyone in the organization participates, and some international organizations actually time-shift the prayer hour to have everyone engaging in the practice simultaneously. It's awe inspiring to think of people pausing to reflect on their mission at the same time all around the world.

At SOF Missions, we stop what we are doing every day at noon to pray. Everyone stops working. We gather together and we pray. We take a moment to reflect both on the cause and how the day's activities fit into our purpose. We don't just pray in silence. We talk. We discuss what we are working on and how it fits into the big picture. We directly reflect on the *why*, which is the ideology that underpins *what* we are doing, so that we don't lose sight of the mission. Our mission is to empower veterans to change their lives and the world for the better. We reflect on how the day's activities fit into and further that mission. If we are on a humanitarian mission, we consider whom we are helping, how, and why this brings the world closer to our vision. We ask questions. We discuss how these missions empower veterans and make the world a better place. We come together in a shared sense of spirit.

This kind of active spiritual formation reminds people not only of the real contribution they are making, but also why they wanted to contribute in the first place. At SOF Missions, we are here to serve. We serve God. We serve veterans. We serve each other. We serve our communities. We serve our fellow man. This sense of service is critical to our ideology, but we sometimes forget how important this work is to our sense of self. Prayer and other practices of reflection serve as much-needed daily reminders that what we are doing matters—and that it matters to us. When we pray for the people we are serving, we keep our service to them centered at every level of the operation, including the daily operations, when it is easy for the grind to wear down one's sense of purpose.

I can see these daily practices boosting team morale. No one is reaping substantial monetary rewards for their work with SOF Missions. Most people are volunteers and the staff are not getting rich. The rewards are the work itself and the results. When we meet daily to pray or meditate, we are able to pause and take stock of what we have accomplished. And because our work is in line with our ideological goals, we feel good about the work we do. Afterwards, everyone feels energized and recommitted to the cause.

COMMITMENT

Ideology means nothing if it is not referenced and practiced consistently. You have to be committed to your ideology or the daily grind will wear you down. Your ideology is your buffer against spiritual deflation. A strong ideological base will protect you from low morale, but only if you're truly committed to that ideology. No one overcomes major challenges or achieves great feats with one foot out the door. You have to be totally committed.

Commitment is not just a frame of mind, but also a set of daily practices, just like spiritual formation. You don't just commit once and you're done. You have to commit, then recommit every day—every moment of every day really. This is how commitment works. It has to, because commitment is not an inherently binding state. As agents with free will, we are capable of walking back on our commitments at any time. This means that commitment is not just a vow, but also the active process of *keeping* the vow.

Consider marriage. Wedding vows are one of the deepest commitments most people make. Wedding vows are serious and beautiful, expressions of commitment to a spouse. But we all have a friend and/or family member who has gone through a divorce. The vow didn't mean a whole lot after it was broken. In a way, the vow really only matters when you are making it. By the time you take that first kiss as a married couple and start walking down the aisle, the vow no longer matters. What matters from that moment and every moment on is commitment to that vow. You live that commitment every second of every day.

Successful marriages are, by definition, those in which you recommit to your spouse every day by behaving in ways that stay true to the vow. Vows are just words unless your actions reflect your commitment to that vow.

And so it is with all commitments. Commitment to an ideology, a cause, or a movement is the same—not just words, not just an action, but a lifetime of sustained action. You have to wake up every day and recommit to the cause and the reason for working toward that purpose. You have to make this ongoing commitment every day, forever, until you stop.

I was a long-distance runner in college. This was a transitional time in my life. I was fleeing the streets of Los Angeles and teen hooliganism for a new life in academia. Running was a spiritually healing undertaking that helped me refocus my negative energy into a positive activity. I committed myself fully to the sport. People ask me, "How do you run a marathon?" And I tell them: "The same way you commit to doing anything. You get up, put on your shoes, and take the first step out the front door." That's it. You put on your shoes and start hammering the pavement, training every day, without fail. Consistency is the key to commitment.

This kind of consistency requires discipline. And I'll tell you what: running a marathon is way easier than trying to establish an organization! Starting a real movement takes the kind of sustained discipline you will only be able to maintain if you are ideologically committed and your mission is aligned with your core beliefs. Building a movement is a serious commitment of time, energy, and resources from both you and everyone you recruit.

If you are pursuing a mission out of a deep sense of purpose, your ideological convictions will make it easier to commit and stay committed. That burning commitment to your beliefs will keep you going in tough times and through the daily grind. It will help you overcome both adversity and mundanity. It will help you get up each morning and fight the good fight.

REST AND RECUPERATION

While spiritual formation is mostly about active practices, some practices aren't always as active as others. And that's a good and necessary thing. No matter how strong your drive, how burning your ideology, everyone needs a break sometimes.

In the military, we get regular R&R, which stands for rest and recuperation. That is recuperation, not *relaxation*, though R&R is relaxing compared to undertaking missions. This is not just time off for vacation. It is time to rest and reset. Taking a step back from your work allows for perspective on the mission. This is a kind of spiritual formation. Thoughtful breaks allow you to reflect on your mission. You can't analyze your performance when you are in the fray. You have to take a step back to get perspective.

Everyone needs to hit the reset button every now and then. This time allows you to come back not only refreshed, but also recommitted. Time spent considering the cause reminds people why they took up the battle in the first place. SOF Missions holds regular retreats for just this purpose. We also take breaks, at least once a year. These are times for people to reflect on their work. We use this time to celebrate successes and acknowledge failures. We use it to show appreciation for the work everyone is doing. People engage in prayer and meditation. They reflect upon the movement, the mission, and especially the *why*. Again, the *why* behind the mission is the ideology—what are we even taking these actions for? It's important to build daily practices into the workday to address this question, but you should also regularly plan breaks that allow people to spend time reflecting on how the mission aligns with their ideological beliefs.

While these aren't proper vacations, the time away allows us to relax and recuperate. Everyone gets tired sometimes. There aren't enough resources, time, money, or hours in the day. There's always more you could be doing. You simply cannot do everything. Sometimes you need to take a step back. You don't want to burn yourself out and just quit. That doesn't help anybody. You need to take regular time off, in which you engage in active reflection, so that you can come back ready to work twice as hard.

So: Rest. Recuperate. Refresh. Rejuvenate. Reflect. Reset. Recommit. And yes, go ahead and relax while you're at it.

TURN OUT, DON'T BURN OUT

The practices and active mindset outlined in this chapter will help keep the movement on course by ensuring that every action is aligned with the movement's ideology. This keeps the movement from straying off course and keeps people turning out and showing up. These practices help ward off disillusionment and burnout.

Ignoring ideological cohesion and the practices that encourage it is a recipe for failure. Eventually, the movement will falter and fail, if it even gets off the ground. I see this all the time. Many movements start as small endeavors by a single person or a married couple. These kinds of organizations often fizzle and lose steam, even if they start strong. I worked with one such organization that was serving the homeless. It started out strong. The founders really wanted to make a difference in the world. They were passionate about the homeless and worked hard to set up an organization. They soon had the humble beginnings of a possible movement, but it failed to ever really ignite.

The failure wasn't for a lack of followers. People heard about what they were doing and started to show up. But everyone eventually got exhausted. The hours were long, both for the volunteers and the founders. There wasn't a lot of money to pay salaries. People started to feel unappreciated and despondent and left the movement soon after joining. The leaders struggled to keep the organization staffed and ended up doing more and more of the work themselves. Eventually, they too got burned out. They became bitter and disillusioned. The founders felt underappreciated, both by the community and by the population they were working to serve. They eventually threw in the towel and shuttered the organization.

The problem here is that, while their intentions were good, they failed to focus on ideology in their daily practices. Eventually, they started to forget why they were even doing any of this. The grind of making the organization run wore them down. They were so focused on *what* they were doing that they forgot *why* they were doing it in the first place. Once this happens, the movement is ultimately doomed.

This can happen quickly or through attrition. You have to remember why you are doing this. You need regular reminders in the form of ideological practices. Don't forget the reason you got into this game. Nurture your ideological foundation. Follow daily practices that remind you of why you are doing this work. Otherwise, you will start to falter when you feel unappreciated for your work.

I don't know anyone who ever started a successful movement because they wanted to feel appreciated. It's great to feel appreciated, and you want to try to make your followers feel appreciated, but sometimes they just won't. Sometimes, you won't feel appreciated. Often this isn't just a feeling, but a reality, and the people you are trying to help really won't be grateful for your effort. You have to remember that this is not why you got into the game. You start a movement to serve and help, not to get social media likes or pats on the back. Many of the veterans we work with at SOF Missions don't want help at first, even though they need it, and they don't appreciate the offer. Sometimes, the people we try to serve through humanitarian missions reject our help.

In the early days of SOF Missions, we undertook a domestic humanitarian mission to help the homeless in New York City. We were partnering with a local group and volunteers to distribute food and blankets. We were trying to help feed and clothe the homeless. We spent all morning making peanut butter and jelly sandwiches to distribute along with clean water and wool blankets. Then we headed out on foot to distribute the supplies.

I was working alongside a young couple just getting into humanitarian work for the first time. This was something of a trial run for them. They were excited to help and make an impact. The first person we came across was a man who was clearly living under a bridge. We introduced ourselves and asked if he wanted food, water, or a blanket.

"What kind of food you have?" he asked.

"I have a sandwich."

"Well, what kind of sandwich is it?"

"Peanut butter and jelly. It's awesome," I said, proud to have made it myself.

He made a displeased face. "Do you have any turkey and cheese?"

Unfortunately, we did not. He turned down the PB&J, though he did take the water. He didn't want the blanket. He said he wanted a cotton blanket, not a wool blanket.

Walking away, we felt snubbed. Here we were, a dozen of us, giving our day over to making sandwiches and handing out supplies, and this guy had the audacity to refuse what we were offering. He didn't care that we wanted to help. He didn't say thank you for the water. He just took it and walked away grumpily. We felt embarrassed for having even made the offer. We felt dumb for wasting our time. Why were we even there if people didn't want what we were offering? Why try to help people who don't appreciate the effort?

For a moment, watching him walk away without so much as a word, I felt angry. We gave our time, energy, and money to be here—and this guy didn't even care. He didn't care for my peanut butter and jelly. My wool blanket wasn't good enough. I was upset! The young couple working alongside me was visibly deflated. I could see that they just wanted to go home. To be honest, I kind of did too.

But only for a minute. I shook it off and reminded myself that it wasn't my place to be upset. I didn't know this man or his motivations. And he didn't represent the entire homeless population of New York. He was just one guy who didn't want my sandwich or blanket. Maybe someone else would. Maybe someone was so hungry that they would love a fresh meal. Maybe there were people who would be so cold at night that they were desperate for any blanket.

And you know what? Other people did want our sandwiches and our wool blankets. We kept going. I sucked it up. I encouraged the couple not to be discouraged, even though I had been, and we found other people to serve. They were happy for a meal and a warm blanket. They were grateful, which boosted our morale, but that's not even the point. We weren't there to feel good about ourselves. We were there to serve and help. If *no one* wanted what we were offering, we shouldn't have been upset—we should have just offered something else.

It's easy to allow your need for validation or other trivial concerns to eclipse the mission. But don't let your ego derail your mission. The point isn't validation. The point is to serve. That's the purpose, always, no matter the specifics of the mission. We are all human, fallible and petty at times, so we have to check ourselves. The best way to do that is to work in these daily practices that keep your focus not just on what you are doing, but the ideological reasons why you are doing it.

If you don't have those reasons locked down, if you aren't engaging in regular practices that keep them centered, you're not going to last. You cannot be doing this for thanks. You cannot be doing it because appreciation or recognition feel good. Wanting to feel good is not an ideology. Hanging out and pursuing hobbies feel a lot better. So does going to the movies or the beach. And those are the kinds of things you'll find yourself doing if you're not being driven by a burning ideological need to do the work and serve for service's sake.

This is an extreme position, but it is the mindset I have adopted. No successful movements ever ignited without an underlying ideological need to pursue the mission. You have to be relentless. There isn't much money in this work. There's not a lot of recognition or fame. You *are* going to struggle. There may be times when you cannot keep the lights on. You will have to lean hard on volunteers and donors. You will often be the primary volunteer and donor for your own cause, especially at first. If you don't have a strong ideological reason for putting yourself through all of this trouble, why do it? If you don't have a good answer now, you won't when it matters, and you'll quit. And so will everyone else who is working with you, assuming anyone is left.

That doesn't have to be your fate. Figure out your purpose. Figure out *why* it is your purpose. Find the texts, the guidebook, that clarify your sense of purpose and why you identify with it ideologically. Adopt organization-wide practices that reflect and reinforce your ideology and foster spiritual formation. Nurture the shared esprit de corps by acknowledging and respecting the movement's covenant. Really commit to the cause on a daily basis. Take time to reflect and recuperate. Live your ideology out in the world, not just in words, but in actions.

CHAPTER 5

PILLAR III: ORGANIZATION: BUILDING OUT THE INTERNAL STRUCTURE OF A MOVEMENT

T he best leaders, even driven by the fieriest ideologies, will not succeed in igniting a movement unless they have the right organizational structure in place. This is especially true of modern movements, which are often sparked by nonprofit organizations. In the past, an organization could grow around a movement. That still happens, but the realities of operating in the modern world mean that an organization needs to form early, often when the movement is still growing.

Long gone are the days when Martin Luther could write his *Ninety-Five Theses* and ignite a movement by publishing and disseminating it widely, helping to launch the Protestant Reformation. The popular image of him igniting the movement by nailing his ideology to the church door is a powerful vision of movement ignition. In Luther's day, back in 1517, he contended with the rules of an all-powerful Catholic Church. Modern movements have to contend with bureaucracy, regulation, the tax code, various laws, and much more.

In this modern environment, people with a shared ideology are less likely to come together and form a movement without an organization to lead the way. The movement is still not the organization—it is the people—but in a modern world of law and legal liabilities, an organization is generally needed to ignite one. Operating in a well-regulated economy within a bureaucratic state requires most movements to organize around and act through a 501(c)(3) nonprofit.

While the organization is not the movement, the organization is crucial. It forms the Third Pillar upon which the movement rests. For that pillar to be reliably loadbearing, your movement has to have a strong organizational structure.

WHAT IS ORGANIZATIONAL STRUCTURE?

Organized movements have both an internal apparatus and external operations. The internal workings of the organization are its *organizational structure*, which is what we will be discussing throughout this chapter. The organizational structure describes the operations, staffing, divisions and hierarchies, training, internal logistics, processes and protocols, chain of command, and all of the other internal structures that allow an organization to run. External operations are expressions of *strategy*, which we will delve into in the next chapter. Strategy is the outward expression of the organization and includes communications, public relations, messaging, networking, external operations, and other processes related to how the organization connects with people and institutions in the wider world outside of its own walls, which is, to reiterate, the topic of the next chapter.

While organizational structure and strategy overlap, as they both describe the function and construction of the same movement operating with a single sense of purpose, the concepts are distinct. However, talking about one without the other is impossible, as they are related. You cannot separate an organization's internal structure from how it operates in the world. They are interrelated. The whole point of the internal structure is to shore up the external operations and messaging.

Don't get too caught up in the details of the distinction between the internals and the externals. The Four Pillars is just a model for grouping the common critical factors of movement ignition into broader concepts that can be thought of holistically. Many factors that make for a strong organizational structure also make for an effective organizational strategy. The factor is the same, but the context is different, and it is important to always consider context. But there's no need to scrutinize the distinctions. The Four Pillars are a loose ontology of interlocking factors. Focus on the broader points. Focus on the factors themselves and the context in which they are being employed.

Now let's consider some of the factors that make for a strong organization, including:

- an effective command-and-control structure suited to the movement,

- effective training and preparation of your people, including the trainers, and

- operation under the three-self Principles that allow for a self-sustaining, self-propagating, and self-governed movement.

We will now look at the finer points of each.

COMMAND AND CONTROL

In military jargon, "command and control," or C2, refers to the exercise of authority and direction of leadership over resources and personnel in pursuance of a common goal. Command-and-control structures encompass a set of organizational traits, protocols, and processes that define how leadership pursues goals with the available resources and people. Command and control is not limited to military use. Any organization with people in leadership, resources to deploy, and goals to be met needs a solid C2 structure.

Command and control is a basic attribute of all organizations. No organization can exist, nor spark a movement, without a command-and-control construct. C2 is simply the way in which commands are issued and missions executed. It is literally impossible not to have a C2 structure. However, if you haven't put thought into designing your C2 structure, it is very likely happenstance and suboptimal at best, and possibly even detrimental and a drag on the organization.

Command and control comes down to communication. Movements and organizations, like the military, are made up of people working toward a common goal. Optimal C2 structures allow everyone to work together in a concerted way. This reduces friction between leadership and subordinates. Communication becomes more fluid. Resources get deployed more efficiently and effectively. The organization performs better.

Command and control is so intertwined with organizational structure that the two things cannot be separated. How communication moves through the layers of an organization determines the shape of and relationship between the layers. Picture an organization as a pyramid with layers cutting horizontally across. The leader sits at the top of the pyramid and hands orders down to the leadership layer below. Each layer oversees the layer below. The bottom layer, the foundation, is composed of the boots on the ground. These are the people who carry out the operations. Everyone above them is in some sort of leadership role.

These layers of command exist for a reason. You want to avoid handing official orders down across layers. This can result in crossed signals and mixed instructions. You don't want multiple people giving conflicting orders. People should know to whom they are accountable and who reports to them. When people bypass the chain of command by issuing orders across layers, signals can get crossed. You can end up creating a situation where someone receives conflicting orders from their boss and their boss's boss. This creates unneeded friction and miscommunication. It also steps on the toes of the person in the middle, who is there for a reason and best understands both the responsibility of his subordinates and the intent of his superior.

The US military exemplifies this kind of structure. There is a chain of command that runs up and down the military, from the grunts on the ground all the way up to the president, who is the commander-in-chief. Beneath the president are the four-star generals in charge of their services. Below them are more generals. Beneath them are colonels who oversee major commands. From there, the chain of command extends all the way down the ranks to the platoon or team level.

As you travel down the chain of command, each layer fans out horizontally, giving the military its pyramid shape. These layers get wider to allow for a *separation of duties*. The foundation is made up by the many boots on the ground, the individual units performing operations, each with their own specific missions and orders.

The people at the bottom are *not* less important. Do not view the hierarchy in an elitist way. Everyone has an important role to fill and deserves respect, especially in a nonprofit, where they may be volunteers or underpaid professionals (as compared to what they could earn in the private sector). The C2 hierarchy is about roles and direction of communication, not a judgment of value. Obviously, people have more responsibilities the higher up they are on the pyramid, but everyone deserves respect for their individual role. In a well-structured organization, there are no unnecessary roles or people.

This structure also allows for decentralized operations to take orders from a centralized leadership. While there is a centralized authority at the Pentagon, which answers directly to the president and Congress, the military is subdivided at every level. Every single person in the military can follow the chain of command up to the commander-in-chief, but the actual work of both leadership and operations is carried out by decentralized divisions. At the bottom of the pyramid, where operations are actually executed, are individual soldiers, marines, seamen, and airmen working semi-autonomously.

This system of command and control is proven. It works. The US military is a well-oiled machine. In my opinion, no other military in history has been so well organized and fluid as the American military. Our C2 structure, second to none, is worthy of emulation, both in and outside of military contexts. Nonprofit organizations can employ the same kind of C2 construct to run a tighter ship, communicate better across a complex organization, and operate at global scales in a coordinated manner. By implementing a clear chain of command and separation of duties, nonprofit organizations can maintain a unified vision while also operating at any scale.

When creating an organizational structure, consider both the vertical axis (i.e., the chain of command) and the horizontal axis (i.e., the makeup of leadership and teams at each level). The nature of the divisions will depend on the scope of the mission and size of the organization. Bigger organizations need more layers within their chain of command and also more separation of duties at every level.

You will be breaking up the organization by both rank and duties. Part of the separation of duties will involve dividing people into physical areas of operation and oversight. If you are operating locally, this could be as simple as putting certain teams or people in charge of specific areas or projects. Big organizations with a national headquarters will also have regional executive offices, as well as local offices. The national headquarters oversees the regional offices, which oversee the local offices.

In *concept*, this is all pretty basic stuff. The trick is balancing the horizontal and vertical axes for optimal results. I am a strong believer in decentralization, which means giving subordinates the freedom to act, guided by the leader's guidance and intent, where judgment and experience require action. At SOF Missions, we strive to have as flat a command structure as possible, meaning fewer layers of command. Currently, we only have three layers, despite operating nationally. We have our small national headquarters, local team leaders, and the team members themselves. The local team leaders report directly to our headquarters. This works because we have a couple dozen teams or groups that we empower nationally. But we are growing fast. Eventually, we will need to establish regional offices. I can imagine a time when we will have multiple teams in each city, local offices, state offices, regional offices, and the national headquarters. If we expand further into other countries, the office in Tampa may become the *inter*national headquarters.

However, we will strive to keep the organization as flat as possible, no matter the size. Needless bureaucracy is not good for an organization. Every layer of command adds more bureaucracy and further removes leadership from the boots on the ground. Decentralization allows an organization to broaden the base of the command-and-control pyramid while limiting its height.

This flatter structure keeps leadership closer to the people actually carrying out operations on the ground, thus lowering the chances that your vision will get distorted as it is passed down the chain of command. At SOF Missions, being in direct contact with every team allows us to communicate my vision directly to the people who are training and leading the boots on the ground. The flatter structure also allows for more specialization at every level. Rather than being divided into redundant and distancing layers of hierarchy, the organization has more lateral divisions. Teams are free to focus on their own communities and missions. This decentralization allows SOF Missions to do a lot of different things and serve many communities in the same organization.

Currently, SOF Missions is serving in more than twenty-five states. Each SOF Team is free to pursue its own mission and sense of purpose. I trust teams and their team leaders to know what their communities need. I trust them to follow their hearts. As long as their operation aligns with our general mission of empowering veterans and those who support them to make the world a better place, I'm indifferent as to whether they are feeding the homeless in North Carolina or leading humanitarian missions to Peru. I couldn't possibly micromanage our teams without hindering what makes each one special and unique. Thankfully, in a decentralized organization, I don't need to manage the teams. I only need to guide, manage, and train the team leaders to understand the organization's purpose and vision.

How flat and decentralized you can get your organization depends on the nature of the mission and your operations. Some organizations will need more layers of hierarchy. The point isn't exactly how many layers you have. The goal is to get your organization as flat as possible while maintaining a clear chain of command by implementing a clear division of responsibilities.

HOW TO BALANCE CENTRALIZED COMMAND WITH DECENTRALIZED OPERATIONS

For decentralization to work and not undermine the chain of command, you have to do three things. The first thing you need to do is provide clear command guidance and intent. The second is to train your people well. They have to know how to carry out their duties on their own. The third is to allow them more autonomy to carry out those duties. Having fewer layers of command means that more decisions can be executed at each level. What you absolutely cannot have in a flat organization is every little thing getting passed up the chain of command. With fewer layers, things pass through the chain of command faster, but the system will become overburdened if every single decision is required to go up. The entire point of an organization's stratifying from the top to the bottom is to diffuse decision-making and responsibilities across the chain of command so that the people on the top don't have to make every decision themselves. If you have fewer layers of command, and you don't want every single issue traveling way up the chain of command, you have to give people the autonomy to act on their own. This is especially important in a very large organization, where lots of decisions are being made and multiple operations are happening at the same time.

I witnessed the problems that lack of autonomy can cause in the US military. Despite being the most powerful and advanced military force in the world, the US military was initially struggling to combat the decentralized terror networks operating in Iraq and Afghanistan. Toppling the Taliban and Saddam Hussein regimes was relatively quick work. Those were centralized organizations. We went in, battered down the enemy, and cut off the head. Squashing the terror networks that sprang up in their wake was much harder. While these terrorist groups didn't have the might or firepower of the US military, they were nimble and flexible. They had no hope of beating us on an open battlefield—but we were no longer fighting on an open battlefield. We were mired in urban combat and guerilla warfare in isolated terrain. These decentralized terror groups were able to mount successful insurgencies that undermined American control and jeopardized the safety of our troops. They couldn't beat us—but we also couldn't wipe them out, not totally, and they remained a thorn in our sides.

The terror networks benefited from decentralization. In Afghanistan, the Taliban no longer had much of a centralized command. We destroyed it. Only the decentralized terror networks remained. In Iraq, we faced the same thing with Al-Qaeda. These terrorist combatants would fan out through cities and in the mountains and emerge to take potshots or set off explosive devices before retreating back into hiding. To fight back, the US military adopted similar decentralized tactics. We employed small squads to carry out tactical missions with precision.

However, the US military will never be as decentralized as these terrorist organizations, nor do we want to be. We have different goals. They were insurgents whose only goal was to create chaos to drive us out. Our mission was to liberate, secure, and rebuild Iraq and Afghanistan, which required a sustained and coordinated presence and effort. The terrorists could simply carry out their attacks and disappear into the woodwork. We stayed around and do the work of nation building and providing security. The US military couldn't exactly shuck off central command, nor would it ever want to do so.

Unfortunately, this made us slower than the decentralized terror networks. This was especially a problem for us in Special Operations, where we were gathering intelligence in pursuance of capture/kill missions. Even when we confirmed a target with our own eyes, we generally weren't authorized to engage without radioing our commanders for clearance. The intelligence would go stale by the time it was pushed up the chain of command and the approval came back down. A confirmed target might disappear while we waited for permission. This was especially a problem with high-value targets, which might require us to wait for approval to come down from Washington.

The problem was military bureaucracy. Intelligence wasn't moving up the chain of command fast enough and orders were coming back down way too slow. Waiting for communications to move through the system took even longer when several branches of the military were working together on a mission, as was often the case with Special Ops. Communications not only moved up the chain of command, there were *multiple* chains of command, each branch of the military having its own. In short: we had a problem with command and control. We needed to be more nimble without sacrificing the cohesion and power of a centralized and strong chain of command.

Things began to change when Gen. Stanley McChrystal took command. Famous for his leadership in Joint Special Operations Command, he first streamlined communications between the upper layers of command, especially regarding intelligence, to tighten the upper ranks of leadership. Intelligence was centralized so that the Army, Navy, Air Force, Marines, and all of the Special Ops branches accessed to the same information. This initiative made the intelligence easier to access up and down the chain of command. This ensured fewer crossed wires and less friction as communications moved through the military bureaucracy.

Second, McChrystal empowered special operation forces, particularly on the ground, with more autonomy. Squad leaders were authorized to execute missions within a set of widened parameters. Squads were now able to react nimbly to changing circumstances on the ground. Intelligence could be acted upon the moment it was gathered. If we were on a capture/kill mission, we were allowed to execute the capture or kill once we confirmed the target ourselves— no waiting on the radio while the bad guys got away. We were well trained and briefed on each mission beforehand. We didn't have to wait for orders that were already given. We only had to radio our commanders in the case of an emergency or an unexpected turn of events. The Pentagon could have fallen off the map while we were out in the field and it wouldn't have mattered—we knew how to carry out the mission to their specifications before we ever left base.

These changes to C2 allowed the military to maintain a tight chain of command while waging the war with a highly decentralized military force. We had all the benefits of decentralization, just like our enemies, while still maintaining the chain of command and the benefits of central leadership. Subordinates had the autonomy to execute the mission in accordance with the *intent* of their commanders. Our training and briefings ensured that we understood that intent and made the right decisions on the fly. But we also had the benefits of centralized intelligence and frictionless communication pathways up the chain of command. Commanders, including upper leadership, could still easily issue new orders, coordinate multiple groups simultaneously, and control operations from afar.

McChrystal, a four-star general who was in command of the entire US military operation in Afghanistan, was, among others, instrumental in developing and implementing this new and improved C2 structure. Upon retiring from the military, McChrystal began encouraging businesses and nonprofit organizations to adopt similar command-and-control constructs. In his book, *Team of Teams: New Rules of Engagement for a Complex World*, McChrystal explains the benefits of decentralization and the importance of autonomy at every level.

If anything, this C2 structure works even better in a civilian context. Military operations are matters of life and death. The benefits of decentralization and autonomy are clear. But, if things do go wrong, lives are on the line. The stakes are generally much lower in business and movement building. Nonprofits that don't operate in dangerous environments reap all the benefits of decentralization without the grave risks of a mistake being made on the ground. Even SOF Missions, which *does* do humanitarian missions in remote locales that can be dangerous, is still not even remotely as risky as chasing down terrorists in hostile countries.

I do not mean to downplay the risks, though. SOF teams, especially mine, operate in far-flung places without modern communications infrastructure. We cannot trust our cellphones and other devices to work out in the bush. In these environments, our people need to know how to handle themselves. They need training so that they can operate effectively and safely. They also need autonomy to carry out the organization's mission according to the vision without needing a direct line of communication up the chain of command, which may not always be available. That line of communication may be slow or severed. But this only bolsters the case for decentralization. Our people are well trained because they have to be.

Proper training ensures that these missions do not descend into chaos. Chain of command remains intact, despite decentralization, because we prepare our people before sending them out in the field. They are properly prepared and know what to do before going in. They are given the autonomy to execute the mission on their own, but they do so within predetermined parameters. They understand what is expected of them. They have the right training. They know how to operate according to the military-inspired logistics and safety protocols that we employ. They don't have to ask what to do next because they already know. If we are building an orphanage in a remote area, they know how to find local contractors and suppliers. They know to only work with people who have the kids' best interests at heart. They know to find land the government cannot take.

This allows our people to carry out missions even if I am thousands of miles away in Florida, deployed to Afghanistan, or simply out of earshot when our communications stop working. They don't need to consult me because they already know my guidance, intent, and the mission. They have contingency plans for every likely occurrence. They know when and where to rendezvous for check-ins. The whole operation runs seamlessly, whether I am there or not, because everyone knows what to do and how to do it—and they have the authority to act.

Empower your people, at every level of your organization, to carry out their role. Show them the vision, explain the mission, and offer them the latitude to execute it autonomously. With clear guidance and solid training, they will make faster, better decisions on the ground than you could ever make from afar. For this to work, you have to hire the right people and prepare them well. They should believe in the mission. They should know your intent and be able to act on it. Do this, and they will be able to act nimbly in response to local conditions while adhering to the organization's practices and values.

TRAINING AND PREPARATION: BUILDING YOUR ORGANIZATION

Giving your people autonomy only works if you train them properly. To make good decisions on the fly, your people need to understand their role in the mission. They have to know their equipment. They need to know what everyone else on the team is doing. They need to be aware of the likely outcomes of their actions and contingency plans for any problems that may arise. They need to understand their entire mission set, which defines all the relevant parameters of the mission. They need to know *whom* they are helping, *what* they are doing, the specifics about *where* they are operating, *when* each step is performed, *why* the operation is being carried out, and *how* to get the job done.

Training is preparation, and preparation is the work of an organization. You have to train and prepare as a team so that you can accomplish the organization's overall mission. To accomplish the mission, you have to understand the overarching strategy. For all of this to come to fruition, you need well-trained people. Never launch a mission unprepared. In the military, we understand that a well-executed mission hinges upon preparation. You train within the organization so that you can execute in the field. As a soldier, I trained at Fort Bragg so that I could operate in Afghanistan and Iraq. The military, as an organization, trained us to fight.

We trained *hard*. The US military is the best military in the world because our soldiers receive the best training, second to none. Even the basic grunts receive rigorous preparation that goes well beyond basic training. Each new rank, position, skill, weapon, and anything else should be trained for. We never send our troops into battle unprepared. They know their role. We have people trained to gather intelligence, people trained in operations, people trained in ground combat, people trained in air combat, people trained in everything. They all know a little about what everyone else is doing. Everyone is both a specialist *and* a generalist.

We became intimately familiar with all of the weapons and equipment on the job. We spent countless hours on the firing range and patrolling in the field so that, when it mattered, we could maneuver collectively on the battlefield and execute the mission. We became adept at using our radios, our GPS and maps, our lasers (yes, I said lasers!). We learned to operate in the night using our night-vision goggles. We learned to operate without them too. We learned to operate under stress, at altitude, submerged, in the dessert, in an urban environment. We ran drills over and over so that, when it came time for the fight, we were ready.

Your domestic nonprofit probably doesn't need to put people through boot camp and years of specialized training, but you do want to make sure your people are ready to do their job and that you provide ongoing support. Set up training programs that teach them the basics and then make sure that they continue to learn on the job. Different positions require different training, of course. People need the skills and knowledge to accomplish the specific mission they are undertaking, whether that is building an orphanage overseas or running a health clinic in the local community.

I will never cease to be amazed by the number of organizations that fail to train their people adequately. But, while I *wish* I could say that this was unfathomable to me, it is definitely not—I've done it myself. I had to learn the hard way not to undertake a mission for which you aren't prepared and qualified.

In the early days of SOF Missions, we launched a disaster relief mission in Haiti. We went around helping people rebuild from the 2010 earthquake. While there, we helped a woman build an outdoor kitchen. She was living in what was basically a shed and needed a place to cook. So our team decided to build her a kitchen even though I hadn't built anything in my life, Legos notwithstanding. To this day, the kitchen is still standing, but I honestly couldn't tell you how except to say that it is a miracle. I have pictures of what we built. It represents the heart to do something good for someone who had nothing. But it definitely doesn't represent a structurally solid kitchen!

Our next mission was to the Andes in Peru. This time, we were building orphanages, and we were going to build them right. I now knew better than to build them myself. We brought in contractors who actually knew construction. We trained our people to help. We did it by the books this time, getting all the proper certifications and building to code. We helped rebuild three orphan homes, not a shed, and the projects went great. We never could have done it without the right training and know-how on the team.

Don't try to do a job you don't know how to do. Don't send other people to do a job *they* can't do. That is a recipe for disaster. You are just setting people up for failure. The last thing you want to do is put a lot of time, money, and energy into something that becomes a burden.

CRAWL-WALK-RUN

Be patient with people as they are learning. You have to learn to crawl before you can walk. Basic training only teaches soldiers the basics. They learn everything else through years of ongoing training and by actually *doing*. You can learn the basics of almost any job in a day, or a week, or a month, or sometimes longer depending on the level of difficulty. Actually, growing into a role is something you do on the job. That takes time. There's no other way to learn the ins and outs of the job in training. You have to train on the job.

At SOF Missions, we train people before sending them on a potentially hazardous humanitarian mission. They learn the basics of the mission, with a special emphasis on safety, but that's only a small part of learning the job. The only way to master something is by doing. After basic training about how to conduct a humanitarian mission, our operators learn on the job, in the field, doing the work. That's the only way they will ever learn to *run*.

This applies to everyone in the organization, not just people conducting humanitarian missions. They have to be prepared, but they also have to grow into their roles. This doesn't happen overnight. Crawl, walk, run—it's a continuum and a learning process every time.

UP/DOWN TRAINING— TRAINING THE TRAINERS

While everyone receives different training for a specific role, training can be divided into two basic types—the *up* and the *down*. The "down" is the training for the rank and file. These are the people doing the actual work. They are delivering services on the ground. The "up" is the training of the trainers.

This occurs at almost every level of the organization. People should be trained by the level of command directly above them. Training the trainers is how the organization empowers its people and passes vision, protocol, processes, values, and everything else down from the top to the bottom. As an organization grows, even a little, you cannot train everyone yourself. Training leadership to train people is the only way you can reach the rank-and-file doers and ensure they carry out the vision to your specs.

Carefully consider whom you put into leaderships roles. Not everyone is cut out to be a leader. Lots of highly talented people aren't good at training or leading. There are ways to promote people and give them more authority without moving them into active leadership. For leadership roles, I try to hire from within the organization. This allows me to better identify people with leadership ability. These people move up the chain of command and into a training or leadership role. These people will shape the organization from the inside out.

THE THREE-SELF PRINCIPLES: BUILDING A SUSTAINABLE ORGANIZATION

This book cannot serve as a blueprint for every organization. You have to decide how many layers of command you need. You have to decide what to do in-house and what to outsource to partners. You have to decide how to handle training. I cannot answer these questions because every mission is different.

What I *can* tell you is what those internal processes and structures should accomplish. While every organization will have its own optimal processes that match the mission, those processes should make the organization effective, efficient, and *sustainable*.

In mission movements, there is a concept called the three-self principle, first articulated by Henry Venn, who was a general secretary of the Church Missionary Society, and Rufus Anderson, foreign secretary of the American Board of Commissioners for Foreign Missions. Both men were influential in the missionary movements of the nineteenth century. The three-self principle—self-governance, self-support, and self-propagation—was established as a foundation for making indigenous churches self-sustaining at the grassroots level.

The three self-principle has since been expanded upon by other movement theorists. It is as relevant today as the day it was conceived. While the principle originated in the missions movement, it can apply to all movements.

Movements should be organized in a self-sustaining manner. This is not automatic. Nonprofit organizations are not money-making institutions. They aren't driven by a profit motive and therefore aren't, as private enterprises are, guided toward sustainability by the invisible hand of the market. While you can run parts of an organization like a business, at the end of the day, they aren't the same.

Being independent and self-sustaining is important to organizations—and not just for survival. The three-self principle keeps organizations from being too beholden to outside support, which can breed dependency and ultimately compromise the mission. Organizations will always need to partner with others, seek out funding, and work with the outside world, but they should be stable enough to remain independent.

PRINCIPLE 1: SELF-GOVERNANCE

While I strongly believe in flat organizations with minimal bureaucracy, organizations do need strong, independent, accountable leadership. Self-sustaining organizations have a system of self-governance that allows leaders to lead while also holding them accountable. Self-governance means that the organization is in control of its own destiny.

This is ultimately your job. As the leader, the buck stops with you—and that's a *good* thing. You get to be in charge. While there are no excuses for failure, only reasons, you retain control over the organization and are responsible for its successes as well.

Self-governance protects against the effects of corruption through money and outside influence as the organization starts to grow. It is your job to make sure that the movement stays true to its vision. People only join movements because they share in the vision. If the vision falters or becomes corrupted, people will start to leave.

Self-governance does *not* mean you have to do everything yourself. You don't even have to lead alone. In the US, nonprofits are required to have a board of directors. They form another level of leadership and governance. They help hold you accountable and provide wise counsel.

The board should be made up of like-minded people who believe in the mission. This does *not* mean you want yes-men. You want board members who will give it to you straight. Their job is to guide you and you want them to actually do so. They are a critical part of the organization's self-governance structure.

Even if you are not an official 501(c)(3) nonprofit, you should still have experienced people to provide wise counsel. I have made some of the best decisions of my life, and avoided some of my worst, thanks to the advice from wise counsel. Learning from those who have gone before you is a much less painful experience than pure trial and error. Learning from your mistakes is good, but I'm sure many people would agree that it's better to learn from *other people's* mistakes. There's no reason to fall on the same tripwire twice.

Board members often bring their own expertise to the organization. Choose board members with relevant expertise, particularly that which you lack. They should be strong generalists as well as subject matter experts. At SOF Missions, we have board members with a variety of relevant backgrounds and experience. We have a senior military officer, a financial expert, a cybersecurity expert, a world-renowned physician, and more. These people work in areas that are relevant to the work we do. Many have experience working in other nonprofits or serving on other boards.

While they all have different backgrounds, our board members all have at least one thing in common: a passion for our mission. They believe in what we do. They care about veterans and bringing hope to families in our communities. This is the most important quality of any member of the organization, be they a board member or a weekend volunteer. We never select board members based on prestige or connections alone. We select board members who will give the organization their best. Board members should be, first and foremost, people who will provide good advice and hold you accountable. This is a crucial part of self-governance, sustainability, and good leadership.

PRINCIPLE 2: SELF-SUPPORT

Self-sustaining organizations should be financially independent. They should have their own resources, funds, personnel, equipment, space and infrastructure, and other organizational necessities. These resources all cost money, the most critical resource of all and the well-spring from which other resources flow. Organizations need money to do anything. No funding, no mission. Organizations need a fiscal plan for remaining financially independent and viable in the face of black swan events.

This does not mean that organizations cannot take outside money. The vast majority do. In fact, most nonprofits get the lion's share of their funding from donors and foundations. Many sound organizations rely on donations for 100 percent of their funding. There's nothing wrong with that. Donations are a viable revenue stream, a crucial one that most organizations will need. Organizations can no more be without donors than corporations can operate without customers. You have to rely on donations. But you shouldn't depend too heavily on any single donor.

Diversify your revenue streams, even within your fundraising structure. Always be on the lookout for more donors so that you don't depend on your current donors too much. This is especially important if you depend on one especially large donor. That is less than ideal, because it may give that donor undue influence upon the organization and mission. You don't want to become beholden to your donors. It's hard to say no to a donor when they can yank your entire operating budget. Don't get into that situation. If you are in it, don't stay there. Diversify your funding sources.

Do not allow the organization to ever be so strapped for cash that losing a donor means shutting the doors. Keep enough cash in reserve to weather lean times or pay for some unexpected costs. Bad things happen. On a long enough timeline, they *will* happen. There will come a day when you will lose a big donor. There will come a day when money you were counting on doesn't materialize. You will someday face an unexpected expense. This is all normal. These situations can turn into a large problem when you don't have breathing room.

The amount of cash you need in an emergency fund will vary depending on your organization's size, operations, and mission. I recommend being able to cover at least six months of operating costs, preferably a full year, with money on hand. Bigger budgets require more money by virtue of being bigger. The bigger your budget, the harder it is to make up for a substantial loss in income. If you are running a shoestring organization on a few thousand dollars, you can make up budget shortfalls more easily. You can dip into personal funds and make up a small budget shortfall yourself. I did that in the early days of SOF Missions. But replacing a donor who contributes $100,000 annually is a taller order for most. The bigger the organization, the more months of operating costs you should have on hand. Organizations big enough to have more than a couple regular staff members, even if they are small or midsize, need at least six months of operating costs locked away in reserve.

You would be surprised how many organizations do not plan for revenue loss. Lots of organizations operate in perpetual crisis mode. They are always a few months from shutting down. They depend not just on donations, but a *steady* stream of donations. This puts you at risk of shutting down or compromising your vision. If losing a donor means the lights are getting shut off at the end of the month, the organization is not independent and self-sustaining.

Being fiscally responsible is not just about the money coming in. You have to also watch spending and make wise financial decisions. Lots of new nonprofits rush into things without understanding organizational finances. The number one mistake that successful organizations make is growing too fast. They are passionate about the mission. When they see a little success, they throw caution to the wind and double down. They overextend themselves and grow too fast when things are going well. Then they hit a rough patch and the whole organization collapses.

Be careful about overextending yourself or growing too fast. Growth is great—but is that growth reliant on funding that isn't guaranteed? What will happen if the money stops? Organizations need to maintain continuity of operations and services. Growing one year only to scale way back the next is a terrible way to run an organization. You end up canceling services and laying people off. This is bad for morale. People will get discouraged and abandon the mission. Donors will see the organization retracting and pull back if they think you are going under, thus accelerating the process. This can happen fast. A thriving organization can enter a death spiral almost overnight by overextending itself. A single black swan event can set off a chain reaction that unravels all of your hard work.

Sometimes things just don't go as planned. When SOF Missions made the switch from just doing direct humanitarian missions to a focus on serving and empowering veterans, we knew we needed to undertake a bigger outreach project. To help veterans, we needed to be able to reach them. We had to get the word out. We developed a multifaceted marketing campaign with our most ambitious undertaking being shooting a film, *Surrender Only to One*. It focused on veterans' issues and served as an outreach tool to get veterans involved with what we were doing.

Our budget for the film was modest until we met a person who promised to connect us with major donors who would help us make a better film. We brought them in on the project and ramped up the budget. Thinking these donations were locked in, we spent $100,000 of the organization's own money just on the first phase of filming. This was *way* over our original budget.

You can probably guess how this ended. The money never materialized. The person oversold us on their connections. They did some good work, but they clearly misrepresented themselves and their network. We bit, hook, line, and sinker—and now we overspent our budget and we weren't even done with filming.

We were in the red—not just on the film, but the whole organization. We spent money that should have been earmarked for operations. The film was compromising the greater mission. We slowed down production and cut costs. We let go of our intended deadlines and slowed down the pace of filming so that we could forge relationships with new donors. We collected donations slowly and built up a pot of money for the film. Rather than spending with the promise of money, we were spending only money we had. Expenditures were budgeted and paid from real money on hand, which allowed us to spend without worry.

Yes, we slowed down. Yes, we had to push back the première of the film, which didn't happen until three years after we started filming. But we were able to do the project on our terms without further endangering the greater financial solvency of SOF Missions.

Operating with only a month or two of money in the bank is irresponsible. So is overextending yourself. Doing so for faster growth, only to have the organization collapse, is counterproductive and does a disservice to the movement. Don't expand if that growth isn't sustainable. Make a plan. Have an emergency fund. Grow slowly and sustainably so that you can deliver services not just effectively, but also consistently.

PRINCIPLE 3: SELF-PROPAGATION

Self-propagation has always been an important part of the mission movement. Early missionaries were setting up churches in new places, usually indigenous communities that had never heard of God. For these churches to endure, they would need to be self-propagating. They weren't engaging in conquest or colonialism. They were spreading the message about God. They were showing people the power and love of God so that they would establish their *own* church. The missionaries helped, but the indigenous people were being brought *into* the church, into the movement, to take part.

In Christianity, and especially the mission movement, there are two related concepts known as sodality and modality. Sodality is the church. Modality is made up of the missionaries who go out into the field. The church stays in place and forms the foundation of the organization. The missionaries are mobile and able to move outward into the world.

This is a tried-and-true formula. We see the same general structure in the military, with the bases forming the stationary sodality and teams sent out into the field to establish combat outposts. In business, you have headquarters and franchises. Successful Christian movements in history operated as modalities of the church. The church was static, but the missionaries went out to form movements. Movements need a modality arm, especially if they want to grow. Without the modality, you aren't out moving and operating in the world.

This is a natural way for an organization, any organization, to spread outward and propagate. At SOF Missions, we employ the same strategy of self-propagation. Many of the veterans who go through our four-phase healing program (The Resiliency Project) join a SOF Missions team. Some establish their own team. They see the difference we are making in their own lives and in the world, and they want to join the movement and do the same.

These teams are self-propagating because they form on their own. We help them get started and provide ongoing support, but they are a sodality in the sense that they go out on their own to take the movement elsewhere. These teams are mostly autonomous and self-governing. We don't tell them what to do. We empower them to make the change they want to see. As long as the team's mission aligns with ours, which is to make the world a better place through service, we don't interfere. Of course, we can always yank their SOF Team tag for violating the agreed upon ground rules, but this has never happened. People who join our movement do so because they share our values and sense of purpose.

Your organization may not involve teams, but you will need to attract people into the movement. As you grow, the organizational structure will have to shift and change to accommodate new levels of hierarchy. This is true of organizations with even the flattest of structures. You will never be able to run a national organization from a single office. You will need people replicating your model if you want to serve more people. These offshoots—whatever you call them—will need to be self-propagating and encourage participation in the movement. That's the only way a movement can be sustainable.

For this to work, you have to have a coherent message. People have to know what you do and why. At SOF Missions, we do three things. One, we spread awareness about veterans' issues and PTSD. Two, we provide support through groups and education. Three, we provide intensive, holistic care for veterans in dire need that includes psychological, physical, and spiritual components.

People have to understand what we do if they are going to get involved. Clear messaging is critical. You don't want people getting mixed signals or the wrong idea. We strive to communicate what we do consistently and clearly. And when we do, veterans want to get involved. They want to form their own SOF Missions team.

How do I know? It happens all the time. We are running more than two dozen teams now and new ones keep popping up. SOF Missions has become self-propagating and thus self-sustaining. This is critical if you want the mission to outlast you, which you should. The movement isn't about you. SOF Missions isn't about me. I'm taking every measure to ensure the movement outlasts me and continues when I am long gone.

THE ORGANIZATION IS NOT THE MOVEMENT

In closing, it is worth restating that the organization is not the movement. The organization serves the movement. The organization is a structured bureaucracy for administering and carrying out the work of the movement. But the movement is the people, bound by a shared ideology, working under strong leadership, working through an organization, to execute on the mission and a strategy for making a specific vision of a better world a reality. The movement is all Four Pillars, not just the organization, and the movement is what ultimately matters.

It is very easy, as a movement grows, to start treating the organization like a business and an end in its own. Don't lose sight of why you are doing this by only focusing on the how. That will inevitably result in the movement veering away from its ideological foundation and, ultimately, the mission that brought it together.

CHAPTER 6

PILLAR IV: STRATEGY: CONTEXTUAL MESSAGING, OUTREACH, AND PARTNERSHIPS

N
o movement is complete without the right strategy, which is the fourth and final pillar of movement ignition. The organization, discussed in the last chapter, is the *internal* structure of the movement. Strategy is the *external,* outward expression of the movement. Anything that deals with the movement's public-facing expression falls under strategy, including how the movement interacts and connects with the target population it serves, donors, and the wider public. Contextualizing the movement's message, learning the culture and understanding its worldview, building relationships with your audience, engaging with donors, using technology, hosting

events, partnering with other organizations, and providing a service are all strategic output. These things define a movement's strategy.

New nonprofits typically operate on shoestring budgets. They can't afford to make devastating mistakes or waste resources. The wrong strategy is your worst possible liability. You'll miss out on opportunities, reach fewer people, attract fewer dollars from donors, and ultimately make less of an impact. You won't do as well or last as long—and you certainly won't spark a movement.

Many nonprofits fail at strategy. Most organizations understand the need for strong leadership, a vision grounded in ideology, and an organization that operates as a well-oiled machine—but all too often they lack the basic fundamentals of strategic output. This is a critical mistake. All four pillars are required for movement ignition. You can't overcompensate for a poor strategy with good leadership, a burning ideology, or organizational strength.

So, what makes a good strategy? Simple. There are a few tried-and-true factors that you can apply to your strategic output, most notably:

- contextualizing your message to those you want to help,

- learning their culture,

- forging strong relationships built on trust and respect,

- offering meaningful services that actually create impact,

- successfully using technology to amplify your message,

- doing community outreach and providing solid strategic output, and

- entering mutually beneficial partnerships with other organizations.

Now, let's examine these factors in detail.

CONTEXTUALIZING YOUR MESSAGE

One of the key components to a successful strategic campaign is contextualization. You need to be able to present the movement's mission to the people you are trying to serve. You can't serve them if you can't reach them. And you can't reach them without "speaking their language," so to speak. You have to contextualize your message in a manner that appeals to the people you want to help by couching it in language that appeals to them. At SOF Missions, all of our publicly available materials and strategic output are contextualized to speak to veterans.

Authenticity matters here. Everything we put on social media is genuine, sincere, and informed. You have to be genuine. People can tell when you aren't sincere. You won't fool people. Don't even try. If you act earnestly from a place of true concern and ideological conviction, it will be self-evident. Just do the work and tell people about it. *Show* them that you understand and care about them. If you truly do and have a heart to serve, your true intentions will show.

A great example of contextualization, of which our team is very proud of, is the film we made, *Surrender Only to One*, as part of our strategic output at SOF Missions. The film features actual veterans talking about their real problems and how SOF Missions helped save them. There is no better mouthpiece for the work that we do than the veterans themselves. In the film, many of the warriors share their experiences with PTSD and suicidal ideation and how they each discovered hope, turned things around, and found healing. They tell stories that other struggling veterans know well, delivered in language that they are familiar with.

The film has helped us reach many veterans who are otherwise unreachable. Many concerned friends and family of struggling veterans tell us that they can't reach their loved one. Veterans are notorious for shutting down when people that don't understand their problems start prying. They won't open up to you unless they think you understand and can help—contextualization is necessary to show them that you understand and care.

This is not unique to veterans. Many struggling people don't want to talk about their problems. They will only hear your message if you communicate it in a way they understand and that appeals to them.

LEARNING THE CULTURE

Learning the culture of the people you want to serve is key to contextualizing your message effectively. Learning the culture also helps you build trust. Many insular cultures of the marginalized, be they poor villages in the Third World or homeless encampments in Los Angeles, don't trust outsiders—and for good reason. Most people don't know a thing about the lives they lead or the problems they face. To be let in, you have to show them that you actually understand their worldview and their needs.

Often, marginalized and struggling communities are badly portrayed in the culture at large. This is certainly true for veterans, who are often stereotyped and misrepresented in the media. This is also common to law enforcement and first responders. In the movies and on TV, you don't see the pain they struggle with. You rarely see the PTSD that results after the battle is over and the credits have rolled. Many veterans feel like no one understands them. They think no one comprehends their pain, and they just shut down. Again, this is why family and friends say veterans can't be reached—but that's not true. You just have to connect in the right ways. You have to speak their language. You have to be able to communicate that you know what they are going through and that you really want to—and *can*—help.

This is easy enough for us at SOF Missions. We are veterans, and family members of veterans, serving veterans. We bear many of the same scars as the veterans we work with. They know we have been to war, to hell and back, and they see we carry the same burden. We speak the same language and know the same pain. In many cases, they can see themselves in us. And seeing that we have found hope and are on a path toward wellness proves that they can do the same thing. They are eager to connect if they can *see* themselves in what we have to offer.

Connecting with people is much easier when you are of the same culture, but much more difficult when you are helping people who are very different from you. When SOF teams undertake humanitarian missions in foreign countries and work with indigenous peoples, we should invest the necessary time to familiarize ourselves with the culture before we ever deploy. We need to show goodwill and respect to earn credibility with them. A large part of this is just respecting their culture and following the norms and rules of their society.

This has worked well for us on our humanitarian missions, such as our efforts in Peru building orphanages and providing aid. I have seen other nonprofits struggle to operate there because they come in without a basic understanding of the culture. I see this same mistake over and over. Whether it is ignorance or laziness, I don't know— either way, it is bad strategy and can lead to failure.

That's not how SOF Missions operates overseas. We take the time to familiarize ourselves with the culture, laws, regulations, and anything else necessary to set the mission up for success. We get the right permits. We reach out to municipal boards and leaders. This has opened many doors to serve populations that we may have not been able to. Our hope is that they can see we have a sincere desire to *serve*, not just help.

Not knowing the culture can lead to misunderstandings that undermine the mission. You might offend people accidentally if you don't understand the local customs and social norms. I learned this the hard way as a young lieutenant in Iraq. After the invasion, I was providing security to a convoy bringing critical supplies to the northern region of the country. The civilian workers transporting the supplies were foreign contractors from other Middle Eastern countries. We were managing logistics and security while they did the hauling. A successful operation meant working together.

Unfortunately, I ruined relations by merely saying hello to a woman in a burka in the foreman's presence. This was a huge faux pas and an insult in their culture. They were both horrified even though I was simply trying to be nice by Western standards. But this wasn't Los Angeles or anywhere else in the United States—it was the Middle East. I messed things up by not understanding their culture.

To get up to speed on the culture and build credibility, you need to do the research and get down in the trenches with the community. The movement and its leaders must be working directly with the target population. That's how you connect and become credible. Do your homework, understand the intricate details of the people you are going to be working with, and learn their culture. The more you get to know them up close and personal, hopefully the better the mission will go.

This is especially true if you aren't from the community. Veterans are more likely to listen to other veterans. The homeless are more likely to hear those who have gone through the same challenges they have. But if you aren't part of the group, or haven't been, you really need to embed with them and intertwine your daily life with theirs.

The homeless will roll their eyes at someone who thinks they understand homelessness because they have a PhD in public administration or social science. But they will listen to someone who has been down in the trenches with them, shows up every day, listens to their concerns, and really understands them. Otherwise, you'll never earn their trust. And if you can't earn their trust, they will never accept your help.

BUILDING RELATIONSHIPS, GARNERING CREDIBILITY, AND GAINING TRUST

Movements are constantly building relationships. Every time you interact with the community in a (hopefully) positive way, you have a relationship-building moment. These positive interactions are critical to garnering community members' trust and goodwill, especially with populations that are often misunderstood. You can't help people who don't trust you, don't find you credible, or don't even know about you. People have to have faith in the work you do. That's true for the US military and it's definitely true for small organizations. You have to gain the trust of the people you want to help.

There are two basic approaches to gaining a community's trust through relationships: a grassroots "bottom-up" approach, and a "top-down" approach in which you gain influence with leaders and influencers to earn credibility with the community.

The bottom-up approach to relationship building requires being down in the trenches. You have to show people that you genuinely want to help and that you are willing to roll up your sleeves and get dirty. This tactic will garner much respect within the community, which ultimately leads to credibility.

This grassroots approach can be as simple as connecting at their level and treating them as equals. It is a direct reflection that you respect their culture and whatever differences may exist. When you are in the trenches, you are a teammate—in the same struggle and in the same fight. When in the military, I sometimes used soccer as a way to connect with the locals while operating in Iraq and Afghanistan. Soccer isn't terribly popular in the US, but it is wildly popular almost everywhere else. We would carry soccer balls with us when we were out in the field. I never deployed without at least a handful of soccer balls. I was once in a village pillaged by Al-Qaeda. We wanted to help and track down the terrorists, but the locals didn't trust us, especially not after what had happened. They just wanted to be left alone. They were much too afraid. We went around knocking on doors, but no one would come out. The streets were absolutely empty. Not a soul in sight.

So, we pumped up the soccer balls and started a pickup game in the middle of the village. At first it was just military guys, all of us in full kit with rifles slung over our shoulders, but eventually kids started noticing us. Then they joined in one at a time. They challenged us to a game and we said sure. They started *crushing* us. They moved like lighting and we were stumbling around in our gear. I sprained my ankle and almost ended up killing myself with my rifle. No one wants to lose, especially us "military elite." But all the training in the world didn't help our Special Forces team against these kids. We lost.

My pride and my ankle were hurt but it was worth it. Soon, the whole village was gathered around. We passed out water and food to spectators. Afterwards, we talked to the adults through our translators and started collecting intelligence on the Al-Qaeda attack. And it all started with a little goodwill and a friendly game of soccer.

Once we connected with the village elders, we could pursue a more top-down approach to developing relationships. First we gained access to and won over local influencers. Doing so allowed us to garner even more trust among the rest of the community. In the military, we often employed a strategy of "key leader engagement," which involved developing relationships with community leaders and influential civilians. Both methods work well and should be used together, as appropriate. The right strategy is always the one that is most effective for a given situation.

It reminded me of a time our SOF Missions team was on a humanitarian mission to Haiti. We were responding to a catastrophic earthquake that killed hundreds of thousands of people. Here we ran into the same problem, so I thought back to my time overseas and decided to try playing a little soccer again. It only took a few minutes before children showed up. Within ten minutes, a full-blown soccer game was on. We lost again and again. I ended up pulling a hamstring trying to keep up. The soccer game led to a rare meeting with the village elder. The doors were opened, and we were able to provide critical supplies to their village—especially the poor. Mission accomplished!

Creating long-lasting relationships is an ongoing process. You can't just set it and forget it. You have to *remain* engaged. You have to *nurture* goodwill and credibility. You have to *uphold* hard-earned trust. People need to believe, and *keep* believing, in your mission and good intent.

DONOR ENGAGEMENT— MESSAGING YOUR IMPACT

You also have to contextualize your message for donors and the wider community. This is going to be very different from how you contextualize the message to the people you are trying to help. With those you want to help, you want to show that you understand their problems, needs, and culture. Donors really just want to see *impact*, which is nonprofit jargon for results. If they are going to give you their dollars, they want to know that the money will be put to good use.

This gets easier with time. While you can never *stop* working on strategy, your efforts will build momentum and the effects will start to snowball. Make a real impact, and people will start talking about you. You want to amplify that talk by clearly messaging your mission and its impact to the wider community and potential donors. Show them the impact you are making and keep that message front and center.

Impact is not something you can fake or exaggerate. It needs to be real. You won't ever create a real buzz and get people talking unless you are actually improving lives. You can't fake this—not over the long term—and why would you? The whole point is to make the world better. Your success will depend on your ability to convey the story of your success and impact to donors, but ultimately, the proof is in the pudding. If you can show that you are making an impact by offering services that people need, you will be more credible and have an easier time finding donors. The more people want and need your services, the more freely donors will give money and other support. When people see legitimate impact, they become believers.

If you are like me, you got into this line of work to make the world a better place. One component of running a nonprofit is fundraising; it's crucial to sustaining an organization and ultimately the movement. All nonprofits need revenue—most get it from donors and foundations, and, depending on your line of work, government grants. Securing funding hinges on trust and credibility with the donor class and your ability to both make an impact and message that impact to donors. Learn to effectively communicate your results. Effective strategic output that showcases your impact is absolutely critical to securing the resources and support you need to do the work, empower your people, and accomplish the mission you have set out to do.

When showcasing that impact, vivid and powerful messaging is everything. You want to clearly communicate who you are and what you do in every strategic engagement with the wider public so that donors can find you. Without clear messaging, how will people be inspired to join forces or support the cause you are passionate about? They won't.

Not all donors and philanthropists will care about your mission or movement. Don't waste time on those who do not share your values and care about your mission—just find the ones that do. Donors give money to organizations that match their values. This seems self-evident, but you want to appeal to people who care about the same things you do. These people are likely already connected to the community you are serving. At SOF Missions, we support veterans. Veterans and those with a personal relationship to the US military are some of our best donors, both in terms of time and also money. Find the donors who care about *your* mission and seek them out specifically—then show them the impact you are making for people or a cause that they care about.

CREATING IMPACT WITH MEANINGFUL SERVICES

You can't contextualize impact you aren't making. You need to offer services that actually make a real difference in people's lives. It is my personal conviction that impact should be measured in terms of how well you help people meet basic needs. The needy and downtrodden can entertain themselves. What they can't always do is access food, clean water, housing, and medical care. I felt called to pursue humanitarian work to help people with these necessities. I started working with veterans because suicide literally claims the life of another veteran almost every single hour. There is no greater impact on the world than saving a life!

Knowing what services to provide is essential. When SOF Missions began as an organization, we primarily focused on conducting short-term mission trips. Before going out, we always assessed the needs of the community and provided the services that were in highest demand. We knew that in order for us to earn trust, build relationships, and make the greatest impact possible, we provided something the community needed. In 2014, SOF Missions traveled to Peru with a group of eighteen workers. The need in the community was great, so we developed a plan to provide a large list of services. At that point, it was the biggest endeavor we'd undertaken so far, but we knew that, if we could pull it off, the effort would be worth it.

The key to providing the services needed for the mission was to bring field experts with us. It's my recommendation to never try to provide a service you aren't qualified to offer. To complete the work on the local community center, I brought in a general contractor and construction workers. To provide medical assistance to the ill, we brought two doctors and three nurses. Overall, the trip was a success and we were able to reach more than a thousand people with our message because we took the time to bring the right services to meet their needs.

Now that SOF Missions serves veterans dealing with both visible and invisible wounds, our services range anywhere from providing counselors, mentors, and physical therapy, to support groups and education. It all depends on the individual warrior. Each person is unique. Not all organizations are able to provide different services though. Some only focus on one, and that's fine. The key is to provide the right service to the right population—and whatever services you provide, do them well.

Make a real difference in the world. Make a meaningful impact. The organizations that most inspire me—Samaritan's Purse, Team Rubicon, International Justice Mission, and Fred Jordan Missions— are just a few that supply basic needs and save lives. They are building community centers and orphanages. They are providing housing and food. They are helping people dealing with injustices, abuse, and oppression. Succeeding at any one of these will improve and ultimately save lives—undeniable, quantifiable results. It's my opinion that there's no greater impact than that.

AMPLIFYING YOUR STRATEGIC OUTPUT WITH TECHNOLOGY

To get your message out to the people you are serving and potential donors among the community at large, you need to be using all of the tools at your disposal. In the modern age, this means embracing technology. The internet allows you to reach millions of people. You need a good website and a social media presence that work together to contextualize your message and get it out into the world.

Some people don't like using new technology. I get it—I grew up before the internet and social media doesn't come naturally to me. But these are powerful tools and not using them will handicap the movement. I have known *multiple* people in the humanitarian field—able and highly educated experts—who started nonprofits that failed to gain traction. These are people at the tops of their field, way smarter than me, but they weren't as successful as they anticipated. So, what did they get wrong? They didn't utilize technology to their advantage. Some didn't even have professional websites, just social media pages, if even that—in 2020! Others had *bad* websites, which can be even worse. Sometimes, poor messaging is even more harmful than no messaging at all.

These people were all a little older and hoping to rely on "word of mouth." What they failed to understand is that word of mouth travels over the internet now. You cannot forgo a website and social media today. They aren't the *only* way to get your message out, but they are among the best platforms at your disposal. Why wouldn't you use them? I knew one person who was prominent enough to appear on television regularly but still didn't have a website! He was making an impact, but not having a website and an online presence meant that he wasn't making as big of an impact as he could have been.

If you aren't online, you simply won't reach as many people. And if you don't have a *good* online presence, you won't win them over. Invest in your website, social media and other powerful tools, such as an e-newsletters, blogs, and podcasts. This can be overwhelming at first, but eventually it will become second nature.

You don't have to be technologically savvy to do this stuff. You don't have to be a master at branding. You just need to prioritize and invest in your strategic output. These days, a few hundred dollars will get you a simple professional website that clearly articulates your mission and its impact. Find a volunteer who is social media–savvy (you probably already have one) and let them run the organization's Twitter and Facebook accounts. You don't have to break the bank to get your message out into the world.

EVENTS AS OUTREACH

Technology isn't the only way to get the message out, of course. Traditional forms of networking, such as events and outreach, are as powerful as ever. At SOF Missions, we hold events that allow us to make face-to-face contact and deliver our message in a personal and intimate way to the community and the veteran population all at once. Events are important as they bring large groups of people together to build new relationships and strengthen those already existing. Events have two joint purposes: gather people together to share the message, and provide a meaningful service. We meet veterans who need help, or the friends and family of those who need help. Events are a great way to both connect with the target audience and deliver a needed service.

When we launched our film, *Surrender Only to One*, we hosted events tied to the release. We have hosted film showings across the country with the two-fold goal of bringing awareness to the struggles veterans have and providing a myriad of services to help them overcome and move into a life of purpose. One component of strategic output is having veterans share how SOF Missions has played a critical role in their lives. One way we do this is to have veterans we have helped take the stage at film screenings and public events to talk about their experiences with SOF Missions. They are able to deliver our message in a contextualized manner so that struggling veterans can see how our services can help. There's nothing more inspiring to a struggling veteran than the story of another warrior who crawled back from the brink of suicidal thoughts and found hope, a new life, a happy marriage, and a loving family.

Another organization that excels at hosting events is Fred Jordan Missions, a nonprofit that works with homeless and downtrodden in downtown Los Angeles. Each year, they host numerous outreach events in which they provide meaningful service and resources, such as Thanksgiving dinners or back-to-school supplies, as a way to garner trust and to give back to the community. The events started small but have gotten bigger as the organization has. In 2017, Fred Jordan Missions fed more than two thousand people during a Thanksgiving dinner event. These are incredible outreach opportunities. Once they build trust with the community, they are able to share their message with those attending the event.

THE IMPORTANCE OF PARTNERSHIPS

Effective strategy is all about relationship building. You will not only need to build relationships with your target community but also other organizations. The relationships you forge with like-minded organizations and individuals outside your own organization can be just as important to the movement as the people on the inside. Partnerships allow you to pool resources, share expertise, capitalize on talent and skill from outside the organization, act synergistically to do more with fewer resources, offer complementary services in the same place, and specialize so that you can focus on what you are good at.

Don't compete with other nonprofits; cooperate. You're not running a business—you're trying to make the world a better place. Like-minded organizations can work symbiotically to provide better services. If you are working with the same population, but offering different services, team up to deliver them collectively. If your organization is feeding the homeless and another is providing free medical care for the homeless, you are targeting the same group. Team up to save costs and provide better service. They could provide free flu shots at your soup kitchen. Maybe they can drop off donations of canned goods. You create a synergy with such a partnership.

What you don't want to do is duplicate services. If another organization is already doing what you want to do, why not do something else? Why not help them? Why not look for ways to offer a complementary service? Why not partner with them to expand service to new areas and populations? You should be working collectively with like-minded people to further the mission, not providing duplicate services. Chances are there is a way to work together on slightly different missions advancing the same cause.

Partnerships allow organizations to outsource parts of their operation to organizations that are better positioned to fill those needs. No organization can do everything. Partnerships allow you to expand services without having to offer them yourself. If the service isn't already in your wheelhouse, there is a good chance someone can do it better anyway.

When SOF Missions first started enrolling veterans in our holistic four-phase healing program, which offers physical, psychological, and spiritual healing, we tried to provide all three treatment phases ourselves. We were operating locally at the time, so we worked with physical therapists and counselors who offered their services to our veterans. Now that SOF Missions operates nationally, we need providers in every city. Suddenly, offering even basic physical rehabilitation and therapy becomes a massive undertaking. Building our own provider network in every city is costly, labor intensive, and not always practical.

Fortunately, there is no need to have our own network of providers and facilities in every city. Other existing organizations already offer rehabilitation suitable for our veterans. By partnering with these organizations and networks, we can get our veterans the care they need anywhere in the country. Now, they get *better* care. Our partners have the facilities, the providers, and the know-how to provide better physical rehabilitation and psychological care than we ever could on our own. We oversee, fund, and coordinate care in a holistic way.

Where we excel is by providing spiritual healing. By outsourcing other services to partners, we are able to focus on the thing we do best. When it comes to offering veterans tools to be spiritually fit, it appears as if SOF Missions is suited for just this purpose. This is where we are able to make the biggest impact. We value a whole-person approach. We get it done.

Partnerships allow for specialization. We have our focus. Our partners have theirs. You should never try to offer services that you aren't qualified to do, but that doesn't mean you should let the need go unmet. Find like-minded organizations that can fulfill those needs and work together. Chances are that you will have something to offer them as well.

My motto is: "Together, we are an unstoppable force for good." Show other organizations you are making an impact, they will be happy to team up.

THE TIPPING POINT

This is also true of donors and the wider community. Many people will support your cause if you can show them you are making a difference in the world. People want to join movements that are making an impact. But you have to (1) actually be making an impact, and (2) be able to effectively communicate that impact to the relevant people in language and terms that appeal to them, preferably by using all of the means at your disposal, including technology, community events, and other outreach.

The military taught me that the right strategy is the difference between winning and losing. You have to win hearts and minds if you want to win the battle. While operating in Iraq and Afghanistan, we earned the trust of the locals in order to help them and to get their cooperation in tracking down bad guys. That trust was mission critical.

For most movements, strategy is the "tipping point" where many potential movements either succeed or fail. Your strategic output and overall strategy need to be on point. As with a sharpshooter dialing in a target on the other end of the battlefield, there isn't much room for error. But, with a solid strategy in place, your organization can find success and message that success to others to help more people, reach more donors, and become an unstoppable force for good.

CHAPTER 7

IGNITING YOUR MOVEMENT, MAKING YOUR MARK

M ovements are ignited when visionary leadership driven by a coherent ideology builds an organization with the proper administrative systems and internal structures necessary to execute effective strategies. Leadership. Ideology. Organization. Strategy. These are the Four Pillars of movement ignition— that's it. This is how you ignite a movement that can change the world, which is by no means a simple or easy feat, but that's how it is done.

This isn't something I just pulled out of my hat. Years of doctoral research went into building the movement rubric that undergirds this book. I studied movements across time and history to determine the critical factors that are common to successful movements. I interviewed leading experts in the mission, movement, military, and nonprofit fields. The book you hold in your hand draws on the wisdom and insights of some of the greatest leaders in history, as well as contemporaries at the top of their fields today. I saw the commonalities that they described in historical movements throughout history, as well as in the US military—which is itself an organized movement—and knew that I was onto something.

The movement rubric, from which the Four Pillars are derived, is just a way to organize the common critical factors into an actionable plan for igniting a movement. The list of factors is not comprehensive, nor are all the factors discussed in this book equally important to all organizations. When applying this book to your own movement-building efforts, you should consider the context in which these factors will be applied, including your specific needs, as well as the tenability of each.

However, while the critical factors don't have the same level of importance in all movements, the Four Pillars themselves are non-negotiable. The common critical factors coalesce around the pillars. Whatever factors are central to your organization, the Four Pillars they make up are always necessary. Each pillar forms an essential leg upon which the movement must stand. You cannot spark a movement without visionary leadership, a coherent ideology, a solid organization, and appropriate strategies. You can't just skip ideology or forgo strategy and expect a movement to spark. Spend time working on each pillar. There are no shortcuts. Movement building comes down to doing the work and doing it well.

BE A MOVEMENT, NOT A MONUMENT

You cannot light a fire, walk away, and expect it to stay lit indefinitely. Likewise, once you spark a movement, as SOF Missions is now beginning to do, you cannot just coast along. You have to keep refining the Four Pillars, shoring them up, and making sure you do the work to keep the movement vibrant. Movements do not always, or even usually, last forever. Sometimes, they spark, only to snuff out when they grow too large or become complacent.

Quite often, this is the result of too much bureaucracy and hierarchy in the organization. The leaders get out of touch with the people as the organization grows. They lose sight of the vision. They start to see the organization as *the* movement, which it is not. The people are the movement. When the organization eclipses the people, you no longer have a movement—you have a monument. The organization becomes a husk of its former glory because the actual movement has died.

The Moravians launched one of the greatest historical movements of all time. Established in 1457, well before the Reformation, the Moravians sought to change Christianity from the inside. They believed that being a Christian was not about doctrine or specific beliefs, but about exercising one's faith in everyday life. They sent missionaries all around the globe to get this message out. They sent missionaries everywhere, even to work with the poor and destitute people of foreign lands, as they believed it was Christ-like to care for the most unfortunate. This missionary work was crucial to the movement, not just the church.

The Moravian church still exists today and reports around 750,000 self-identifying followers. While they still do missionary work, their missionary program is nowhere on the same scale that it once was. Today, the Moravians are more of a denomination than a true movement. There's nothing wrong with being just another denomination but it's not the same thing as a true movement. The Moravian missionary movement is no longer central to the Moravian church.

In more modern times, we often see movements collapse when the organization supporting it becomes a bureaucracy. When the organization starts being run too much like a business, it becomes a business. People often say you have to run a nonprofit like a business, which is true to an extent, but *only* to an extent. The purpose is not to make money. People aren't donating, volunteering, advocating, and working long hours for lower pay than they could make in the corporate world for no reason. They do it because they believe in the mission. If the mission no longer comes first, the movement can collapse even when the organization remains. But that organization is merely a monument, not a movement.

Don't let bureaucracy stifle the mission or choke off enthusiasm. Don't let the organization stray from its vision or ideology. Don't, as the leader, allow yourself to lose the passion or vision that guides the movement—if you do, you may be better off passing the reins on to the next generation of leaders. Don't stop implementing an effective strategy that clearly and effectively messages the impact you are making in the world. If you do, the movement will falter. The Four Pillars have to stay upright for the movement to stay on course.

YOUR PEOPLE NEED YOU—DON'T DELAY

I hope you have found this book helpful. It has been for me. The research that went into this book allowed me to grow SOF Missions and create a greater impact than I ever could have imagined. I wanted to see what makes movements tick, what makes them ignite, and apply the successes of those that came before to my own mission. That mission has changed over time. What started as a desire to serve the poor, the orphaned, the widowed, and the oppressed has morphed into a movement that harnesses the healing power of service to help save our veterans. We are really only just getting started, but a movement has been born.

The same methodology can work for you, too. Whether you are just starting out in the nonprofit world or already running an organization and just looking to run a tighter ship, I hope that the insights and information in this book help you build a stronger movement as well.

At this, I wish you the best—and Godspeed. Because the world needs you. No one can save the world on his or her own. No one movement can save the world. We need many vibrant movements in the world, each pursuing their own vision of a better world. Together, we can win. We can build a better world. We could end hunger and poverty today if we all joined in and played our part. We could end exploitation and abuse and oppression. We all need to come together, not just as nations, but also as a globe, as the human race.

But we can't all do the same thing—there are countless missions that need to be undertaken, innumerable battles and just wars to fight. In today's world, we need all the movements we can get. There have been numerous movements ignited across the span of human history, some big and some small, some that lasted centuries and others that disappeared after months or years, but they all left the world better than they found it. They all made a positive impact because that's what movements do. They make the world a better place in their own way.

You too can make the world better—if you really want to. Honestly, I know that not everyone has the desire, or cares enough to, or is willing to make the necessary sacrifices of time, energy, and resources. But if you are, you can change the world—and I do mean *you*. I believe that God gives everyone gifts and talents, which I like to call "superpowers," that can help transform lives and make the world a better place. We all have something meaningful to contribute. We all have a superpower. Find yours and put it to work helping others. Your superpower might be a useful skill or expertise, resources that you can put toward a mission, or the vision and leadership to lead a movement. Whatever your superpower is, don't waste it.

And don't delay. There will always be reasons to wait until tomorrow, until that next paycheck, until you are more secure, or have more time. These are just excuses. If you really want to help people, then start helping now. If you are reading this book, you already have more time, money, resources, and opportunities than most people. There's no shame in success or fortune, but the fortunate have a responsibility to help the less fortunate. I get it: not everyone has that conviction. But that's mine. I think it's God's as well. If He gave you a superpower, it is to be used to make His creation a better place. We all have a duty to help those who are unable to help themselves.

I really believe that. The world has given me so much, and I want to give back. I was born and raised in Los Angeles. My family lived in the projects. We had nothing but each other. Today, this great nation has given me a noble career, a solid community, faith, a loving family, and even my very *life*. I was on the brink of losing everything. Like so many veterans, I came back from war ready to end it all. But rather than becoming another statistic, I found hope and a reason to live. It kills me inside to know that so many warriors and defenders of this great nation don't find that hope in time.

We are seeing a suicide epidemic. Another veteran commits suicide every hour. SOF Missions exists because I wanted to know what it would look like if, instead of losing another twenty warriors every day, we lost *zero*. But I didn't just imagine that better world—I set out to make it a reality.

What do you care about? What's your vision? You probably already have one. That's great, but stop dreaming and start doing.

Being a visionary only gets you so far—you have to eventually be a doer. Forget the excuses, resist inertia, and get going.

I used to be a long-distance runner. People would always ask me how you run a marathon. Well, it's simple. You have to do two things. The first is to put on your shoes and hit the pavement. The second is to take the next step. That's it. Keep putting one foot in front of the other and you will get to the finish line. The twenty-six miles ahead of you are always traversed one step at a time—as long as you take that first step, and then the next.

Movement building is like running a marathon. You get started and focus on the task at hand. Thinking about ending world hunger is overwhelming. Feeding the hungry people in your neighborhood is more manageable. Helping feed the homeless people on the way to work is something you can do today. You just have to reach into the pantry, get out the bread, and start making sandwiches.

Small differences add up. You change the world one life at a time. Together, *we are an unstoppable force for good.* Movements of determined people can make the world a better place. But we all have to do our part.

Godspeed!

ABOUT SOF MISSIONS

HISTORY

SOF Missions was founded in 2011 by Damon, a twenty-year retired special ops veteran, and Dayna Friedman as a humanitarian missions organization serving over 90,000 people globally. In 2014, SOF Missions shifted focus to provide a high level of specialized care to the veteran community with a concentration on suicide prevention.

VETERAN CRISIS

Over 2.7 million men and women have been deployed to Iraq and Afghanistan in the fight on terrorism. Unfortunately for many, the rigors of combat and the challenges of military service take a toll on their overall health. The suicide rate among veterans has reached drastic proportions. The Department of Veterans Affairs Suicide Data Report from 2019 states that over twenty veterans take their lives every day and the suicide rate for veterans is 1.5 times the rate for non-veteran adults. SOF Missions is committed to combating this problem by empowering warriors to find purpose and be resilient.

OUR SOLUTION

We serve all post-911 veterans who are struggling with the visible and invisible scars of war. We develop and provide customized care for veterans through our national network of partners. Our program, The Resiliency Project, is a holistic and individual focused plan that covers physical, spiritual, social and psychological modalities. Partners in our project include non-profit organizations, veteran mentors, and civilian healthcare providers.

For more information, visit: www.SOFMissions.org